THE JOY OF JOB

DISCARD

An Investigator's Perspective on the
Most Righteous Man on Earth

MARIBETH VANDER WEELE

THE JOY OF JOB

*An Investigator's Perspective on the
Most Righteous Man on Earth*

An Extraordinary Story of
Repentance and Restoration

*"He will yet fill your mouth with laughter
and your lips with shouts of joy."*

—BILDAD TO JOB

Job 8:21

SAGERITY
Discern Press™

Sagerity Press^LLC
P.O. Box 408190
Chicago, IL 60640-0005
E-mail: info@joyofjob.com

For more information about this book, visit www.joyofjob.com.
ISBN: 978-1-7322408-1-0

To Elizabeth Vander Weele,
My Mother and Cherished Friend

To Dr. Harold Vander Weele,
My late Father, a Man of Few Words but Many Deeds

❦

The cover of *The Joy of Job* depicts the author's
late father, from whom she learned the value of the
throwaway line, a key to unlocking the mysteries
of Job. Her father's expression, captured at age 82,
conveys living with joy in one's old age. Like Job,
his journey ended well. The drawing was created
by the author's sister, Susan Vander Wey of Tweed,
Ontario, Canada. Her work can be viewed at
www.pastelpaintings.ca

Acknowledgments

The author respectfully acknowledges that the story of Job is a pillar of multiple faiths. However, this book is written from a Christian perspective, based on Biblical Scriptures. As *The Joy of Job* evolved, pastors, church leaders, and friends supported its development and birth. Special thanks for the encouragement provided by the Reverends David and Maureen Freshour of Chevy Chase Baptist Church in Washington, D.C. Through God's providence, they were the first to sign on to the premise of the book. Thank you to the Rev. Dr. Daniel Meyer, who welcomed me into Christ Church in Oak Brook, Illinois, reviewed the book, and blessed it, and to Mark Lundgren, founder of Secure Church, who greatly encouraged the book's publication. Welcomed support and insights came from the Rev. Dr. John Sittema, a pastor for more than 39 years in the Christian Reformed and Presbyterian churches and retired President and Chief Executive Officer of WorldServe Ministries. He is also my cherished cousin. Thank you also to the Rev. Dr. Daniel Block, Gunther H. Knoedler Professor Emeritus of Old Testament, Wheaton College, who assisted in the translation of a difficult verse and provided alternative viewpoints. Thank you, also, to Ken Stodola, Senior Pastor of Open Door Baptist Church in Prattville, Alabama, for his suggestions and support. Thank you to Coretta McFerren for late-night inspiration, to Admiral Samuel Sax for insightful discussions, to Ted DeRose for his points and counterpoints, and to Dr. Myrna Grant, Professor Emerita, Wheaton College Graduate School, and the author of 18 books. Special thanks to Nancy Moffett, who meticulously proofread the book and each of its verses. I am grateful to the kind contribution of her and many others.

Table of Contents

Introduction

I learned the value of the throwaway line from my late father, a man of few words. At our family reunions, amidst heated debates over politics, my father would listen quietly. Then he would find an opening and, with one meaningful sentence, masterfully challenge an entire line of arguments. A hard worker supporting seven children, my Dutch-American father lived through actions, not words.

Now, years later, as a member of the corporate investigations profession, I teach the value of the throwaway line. It is a brief thought thrown over the shoulder at the conclusion of an investigative interview after notebooks and computers are packed away and everyone is about to leave. The interviewee has suppressed the thought throughout the entire conversation but, consciously or subconsciously, he can no longer hold it in. The words only hint at truth, but the hint contains the key to a matter.

The line has no context.

A throwaway line may be, "And I don't know how he did all that snow plowing anyway," uttered after an investigative interview that has nothing to do with snow plowing. The investigator follows the clue and finds that the company in question fraudulently billed for plowing snow at hundreds of sites, many of which had no parking lots.

The ancient Biblical book of Job is filled with throwaway lines that leave quiet, but unmistakable, clues to the mystery of a suffering man whose story has confounded God followers for generations. The clues are part of an extraordinarily skillful undertaking by the author to teach the reader to "test" a person's words.[1] For unraveling the mystery and powerful message of the book of Job requires a keen understanding of human nature and the gift of deciphering intentions. The investigative profession is skilled in this craft—and detecting throwaway lines is only one of its tools.

There are others.

Investigators learn to set aside the "metaview," or lens through which we initially see a person. Doing so prevents preconceptions about his or her character or reputation from coloring the fact-finding process. We also know that the longer a person talks, the more likely truth will come out. When one is in pain, initial attempts to be brave or noble give way to an outpouring of one's soul.

When we hear a person's version of events, we don't take it at face value. We listen for conflicting or inconsistent statements. We look for contradictory evidence from witnesses. We map out the described sequence of events, using logic to determine if the chronology rings true.

We are also attuned to projection, when a guilty person desperately tries to deflect criticism by accusing others. To disarm the listener, he takes a righteous stand against the very type of misdeeds of which he himself is guilty. Distinguishing

---

1. Job 34:3: "For the ear tests words as the tongue tastes food." Job 12:11: "Does not the ear test words as the tongue tastes food?"

guilt from innocence requires exacting work, and the guilty person counts on the unwillingness of the judging party—an investigator, friend, boss, or relative—to take the time to determine who is telling the truth when the same accusation is leveled at both sides.

Investigators also recognize the more innocuous practice of telling stories about a mythical third party in the same situation as the listener in an attempt to convey truth. This device is used throughout the book of Job. We know that the story is a veiled reference to the listener when the listener accepts it as such.

Investigators can also sense fear and insecurity, which drive pride and demand extreme loyalty from followers, even if it means following a leader to destruction. Detecting delusion is another tool, described in greater detail at the end of this book. Whether a person—or a leader, as in the case of Job— views himself realistically provides a window to the soul.

In requiring this type of acumen, the author of Job encourages readers to be discerning about leadership and not to unquestioningly accept at face value who a person represents himself to be.

The author of Job quietly, amidst the blustery and heated debates, implores us to be wiser than that.

Job was a famously righteous and wealthy leader who endured immense suffering after Satan dared the Lord to a contest of sorts. The Bible says Job feared God and shunned evil. One day, the angels presented themselves to the Lord, and Satan came with them.[2] The Lord pointed out that there was no one on earth like Job. But Satan attributed Job's righteousness to his being blessed by God, arguing that it is easy to be grateful and upright when one has vast wealth. Satan challenged God to strike Job and predicted that Job would curse God, an act that would have hurled the greatest man in the East into Satan's domain and ultimate possession.

In a mystery that has haunted mankind throughout the ages, the Lord agreed to the pact. So began an excruciating test for Job. He lost his ten children,[3] his servants, and his vast herds in a series of catastrophes, caused by both acts of nature and by marauders. Eventually, Job lost his health, too.

After months of suffering, deep grieving over his losses, angry debates with four friends about the nature of God and suffering, and a confrontation with the Lord himself, Job found healing. He fathered a new family, his fortunes were restored, and God gave him twice what he had before. He lived for nearly a century and a half after his restoration. In the end, Job emerged from his grief to discover joy.

As a child, I was taught that the lesson of Job was that innocent people—even the most righteous people on earth—can suffer without reason. God's ways are without

---

2. Job 1:6: "One day the angels came to present themselves before the Lord, and Satan also came with them."

3. Job 1:2: "He had seven sons and three daughters . . . ." Job 1:18-19: "While he was still speaking, yet another messenger came and said, 'Your sons and daughters were feasting and drinking wine at the oldest brother's house, when suddenly a mighty wind swept in from the desert and struck the four corners of the house. It collapsed on them and they are dead . . . .'"

comprehension. We must simply accept the mystery and obey. Left unsaid was the unnerving sense that Job, an utterly righteous man, was the victim of a cruel cosmic battle in which humans were pawns in the game. Which is exactly how Job saw it. In Job 9:17, he spoke about God, saying:

> He would crush me with a storm and multiply my wounds *for no reason*.[4]

Although none of us dared to say it aloud, it seemed that God was capricious in allowing Satan to test Job for their mutual amusement. And if God were capricious, He could not be trusted. For years, I had no way to resolve the incongruity between the harsh and distant God of the book of Job and the loving and trustworthy God I knew.

Then one day, I opened my Bible to Chapter 29. A window opened, permitting me to peer, for the first time, into the unfiltered intentions of Job's heart. This was the first clue to the ancient mystery. More followed. I began to recreate the events of the book and run a movie of them in my mind. I looked at witness statements. I analyzed each accusation. In the heated debates about God's injustice and Job's innocence, I recognized the worst failings of people I have known— and I recognized my own. Startling throwaway lines, hidden without context amidst the bluster, leaped off the pages. The author, with a wink of the eye, had placed clues in plain view.

I now faced a choice: I could ignore these clues and cling to my traditional understanding of the book of Job—and thus join with Job in accusing God of being capricious and cruel—

---

4. Emphasis added by author.

or accept them, placing not God's character into question, but Job's.

I chose the latter. What I found was a masterpiece of a book that communicates one of the greatest stories of forgiveness and restoration ever told.

Chapter 1

REPUTATION

"They waited for me as for showers
and drank in my words as the spring rain.
When I smiled at them, they scarcely believed it;
the light of my face was precious to them."

—JOB
Job 29:23-24

I magine being a newcomer in a place of worship when you overhear two men speaking together. One of them says:

"Hey, did you notice that when I walk through services, people part to make a path for me?"

Intrigued, you edge closer. This must be a powerful man, you think. Is he a preacher? A rock star? A politician? A sports hero?

"Everyone stops talking when I enter the room. They hang on my every word. I'm the wisest person around," he says. "And look: When I smile at them, they can't believe they came this close to me!"

Did he really say that?

If he were a preacher or politician, would you like him? If he were a famous musician, would you respect him? If he were a sports champion, would you want your son or daughter to emulate him? Most importantly, would you leave thinking that someone so fixated on his own acclaim—someone who so loved the stage of human approval—was truly righteous? Yet, these are the sentiments of Job who, in Chapter 29, Verses 7-11, recalls his way of life before catastrophe afflicted him:

When I went to the gate of the city and took my seat in the public square, the young men saw me and stepped aside and the old men rose to their feet; the chief men refrained from speaking and covered their mouths with their hands; the voices of the nobles were hushed, and their tongues stuck to the roof of their mouths. Whoever heard me spoke well of me, and those who saw me commended me.

Job continues in Verses 21-24:

People listened to me expectantly, waiting in silence for my counsel. After I had spoken, they spoke no more; my words fell gently on their ears. They waited for me as for showers and drank in my words as the spring rain. When I smiled at them, they scarcely believed it; the light of my face was precious to them.

To New Testament readers, Job's opinion of his own importance sounds familiar. Jesus described the teachers of the law and the Pharisees in a similar way.

Everything they do is done for people to see . . . . they love the place of honor at banquets and the most important seats in the synagogues; they love to be greeted with respect in the marketplaces and to be called "Rabbi" by others.[5]

The Bible instructs God's followers to glorify God,[6] and the Lord states in Isaiah 42:8, "I will not yield my glory to another," but Job focused on another type of glory: his own. In one of the book's obscure but powerful throwaway lines, Job explained, simply, that he expected that his own glory would not fade.[7]

But fade it did, and in all that he lost—children, wealth, and power—Job was fixated most on one particular type of loss: his loss of reputation. Job said he was humiliated,[8] jeered at,[9] and ridiculed, even by little boys.[10] Young men whose fathers he would have disdained to put with his sheep dogs mocked him in song.[11] Mockers surrounded him and were hostile toward him.[12] They detested him and spit in his face.[13] They struck his cheek in scorn.[14] He had become a laughingstock to his friends,[15]

---

5. Matthew 23:5-7.
6. Romans 15:6: "So that with one mind and one voice you may glorify the God and Father of our Lord Jesus Christ."
7. Job 29:20: "[I thought] my glory will not fade."
8. Job 19:5: "If indeed you would exalt yourselves above me and use my humiliation against me . . . ."
9. Job 16:10: "People open their mouths to jeer at me . . . ."
10. Job 19:18: "Even the little boys scorn me; when I appear, they ridicule me."
11. Job 30:1: "But now they mock me, men younger than I, whose fathers I would have disdained to put with my sheep dogs." Job 30:9: "And now those young men mock me in song; I have become a byword among them."
12. Job 17:2: "Surely mockers surround me; my eyes must dwell on their hostility."
13. Job 30:10: "They detest me and keep their distance; they do not hesitate to spit in my face."
14. Job 16:10: "They strike my cheek in scorn and unite together against me."
15. Job 12:4: "I have become a laughingstock to my friends, though I called on God and He answered—a mere laughingstock, though righteous and blameless!"

and even his intimate friends detested him.[16] His dignity was driven away by the wind.[17] Success had also been driven from him.[18] He was full of shame.[19]

Job sorely missed his own adulation. Despite his initial reverent words[20] and a heroic refusal to stop believing in a powerful God—a choice that has been rightly venerated throughout the centuries—Job was devastated by his loss of prestige, a loss he blamed on God. It was God who had stripped him of his honor and removed the crown from his head.[21] It was God who made him a byword to everyone, a man in whose face people spit.[22] It was God who had wronged him.[23]

Lamenting loss of stature is an understandable human reaction in times of devastation, but it is not that of a righteous man filled with the Spirit of God. The proud nature disdains shame most of all, says William Gurnall in his landmark book, *The Christian in Complete Armour.*[24]

---

16. Job 19:19: "All my intimate friends detest me; those I love have turned against me."
17. Job 30:15: "My dignity is driven away as by the wind . . . ."
18. Job 6:13: "Do I have any power to help myself, now that success has been driven from me?"
19. Job 10:15: "For I am full of shame and drowned in my affliction."
20. Job 2:9-10: "His wife said to him, 'Are you still maintaining your integrity? Curse God and die!' He replied, 'You are talking like a foolish woman. Shall we accept good from God, and not trouble?' In all this, Job did not sin in what he said."
21. Job 19:9: "He has stripped me of my honor and removed the crown from my head."
22. Job 17:6: "God has made me a byword to everyone, a man in whose face people spit."
23. Job 19:6: "Then know that God has wronged me and drawn his net around me."
24. William Gurnall, *The Christian in Complete Armour,* (Reprinted by First Rate Publishers, Volume 1, 1662). The reprint does not provide page numbers. John Newton, the converted slave trader, reportedly said that if

In contrast, the Apostle Paul relinquished his reputation as a wise and powerful religious leader to take on the sufferings that would lead him and others into the knowledge of Christ.[25] Paul no longer sought the praise of man. He had no need to garner approval like a rock star from the powerful.[26] In fact, Paul stated that if he were trying to please people, he could not serve Christ.[27] Other Apostles also rejoiced because they had been counted worthy of suffering disgrace for Christ's name.[28]

Although Job mourned the loss of his path "drenched with cream" and the rock that "poured out for [him] streams of olive oil,"[29] Abraham willingly left his home country for the unknown land of Canaan.[30]

---

he were confined to one book beside the Bible, he would choose *Christian Armour*. Charles Spurgeon commented that Gurnall's work is "peerless and priceless; every line full of wisdom. The book has been preached over scores of times and is, in our judgment, the best thought-breeder in all our library." https://en.wikipedia.org/wiki/William_Gurnall

25. 2 Corinthians 11:24-28: "Five times I received from the Jews the forty lashes minus one. Three times I was beaten with rods, once I was pelted with stones, three times I was shipwrecked, I spent a night and a day in the open sea, I have been constantly on the move. I have been in danger from rivers, in danger from bandits, in danger from my fellow Jews, in danger from Gentiles; in danger in the city, in danger in the country, in danger at sea; and in danger from false believers. I have labored and toiled and have often gone without sleep; I have known hunger and thirst and have often gone without food; I have been cold and naked. Besides everything else, I face daily the pressure of my concern for all the churches."

26. Galatians 2:6: "As for those who were held in high esteem—whatever they were makes no difference to me; God does not show favoritism—they added nothing to my message."

27. Galatians 1:10: "If I were still trying to please people, I would not be a servant of Christ."

28. Acts 5:41: "The apostles left the Sanhedrin, rejoicing because they had been counted worthy of suffering disgrace for the Name."

29. Job 29:1-6: "How I long for the months gone by . . . when my path was drenched with cream and the rock poured out for me streams of olive oil."

30. Genesis 12:5: "He took his wife Sarai, his nephew Lot, all the possessions they had accumulated and the people they had acquired in Harran, and they set out for the land of Canaan, and they arrived there."

Consider Moses, one of the great men of faith whose journey is recounted in Hebrews 11, the book of faith heroes in which Job is notably absent. Moses, by faith, walked away from the honor and riches of being in the household of the powerful Pharaoh. "He chose to be mistreated along with the people of God rather than to enjoy the fleeting pleasures of sin. He regarded disgrace for the sake of [the promised] Christ as of greater value than the treasures of Egypt, because he was looking ahead to his reward."[31] When instructed by God to lead the Israelites out of Egypt, Moses did not believe himself worthy to undertake such a task.[32]

Job, in contrast, saw himself not only as eminently worthy of leadership, but *entitled* to praise for one reason: *because* he rescued the poor and the fatherless.[33] "I put on righteousness as my clothing; justice was my robe and my turban," he recalled of his former way of life.[34]

"Whoever heard me spoke well of me, and those who saw me commended me," Job recalled. Job's statement raises a pressing question: Was it accurate?

Evidence suggests it was not.

First, Job's claim of universal regard is, on its face, unrealistic. What leader garners universal acclaim? Even the

---

31. Hebrews 11:24-26.
32. Exodus 3:11: "But Moses said to God, 'Who am I that I should go to Pharaoh and bring the Israelites out of Egypt?'"
33. Job 29:11-12: "Whoever heard me spoke well of me, and those who saw me commended me, because I rescued the poor who cried for help . . . ."
34. Job 29:14.

wisest and holiest leader in the world, Jesus Christ, faced a murdering crowd consumed by jealousy. Furthermore, like any great leader, Job would have made difficult decisions that left some people angry. His wealth would have attracted naysayers and envious critics.

Second, a highly regarded man in power garners sympathy—not contempt—after he faces tragedy. Think of a great leader who suffered a disaster not of his own making, a leader such as U.S. President Franklin Roosevelt, who was stricken with polio. Although the extent of his disease was not fully known, the public knew he had been afflicted. Did such a disaster decrease his stature? No, experience tells us that heroes who face adversity gain more—not less—respect from their adoring people. How then could family, friends, the chief men, servants, his community—everyone—drop Job like a hot potato when this good man ran into trouble that he did not create? Why were those pearls of wisdom he boasted about no longer in high demand?

Third, Job's claim that everyone spoke well of him for rescuing the poor is contradicted by his own description of skirmishes he had with a group of starving young men living among the rocks. These young men detested him—and the feeling was mutual.

Fourth, the only friends who visited Job forcefully contradicted his claims of blamelessness. When Eliphaz the Temanite talked to Job, nearly the first words out of his mouth were, in effect, "You reap what you sow."[35] Zophar

---

35. Job 4:8: "As I have observed, those who plow evil and those who sow trouble reap it."

the Naamathite said that God had even forgotten some of his sins.[36] Elihu, son of Barakel the Buzite, begged Job to return from evil.[37] Bildad the Shuhite concurred. All four agreed: Job was not blameless.

As we shall see, Job eventually came to realize this himself.

---

36. Job 11:6: "Know this: God has even forgotten some of your sin."
37. Job 36:21 (NLT): "Be on guard! Turn back from evil, for God sent this suffering to keep you from a life of evil."

Chapter 2

INNOCENCE

"I will defend my integrity until I die."

—JOB

Job 27:5 (NLT)

Job's preoccupation with his loss of stature was matched in intensity only by his fixation on being proved innocent. He had done nothing wrong, he maintained. He was blameless.[38]

By Job's account, he hadn't walked in falsehood, nor had he been deceitful.[39] He hadn't concealed sin in his heart.[40] He hadn't been enticed by a woman.[41] He hadn't put his trust in gold,[42] nor did he rejoice over the fortune that his hands had gained.[43] He did not worship the sun or moon.[44] He did not

---

38. Job 31:6: "Let God weigh me in honest scales and He will know that I am blameless . . . ."
39. Job 31:5: "If I have walked with falsehood or my foot has hurried after deceit . . . ."
40. Job 31:33: "If I have concealed my sin as people do, by hiding my guilt in my heart . . . ."
41. Job 31:9: "If my heart has been enticed by a woman, or if I have lurked at my neighbor's door . . . ."
42. Job 31:24: "If I have put my trust in gold or said to pure gold, 'You are my security,' . . . ."
43. Job 31:25: "If I have rejoiced over my great wealth, the fortune my hands had gained . . . ."
44. Job 31:26-27: "If I have regarded the sun in its radiance or the moon moving in splendor, so that my heart was secretly enticed and my hand offered them a kiss of homage . . . ."

rejoice over his enemy's misfortune or curse him.[45] He hadn't denied justice to his servants.[46] He hadn't failed to pay for the yield of his land, nor did he break the spirit of its tenants.[47]

He hadn't denied the desires of the poor or let the eyes of the widow grow weary.[48] He shared bread with the fatherless, rearing them from his youth[49] and rescuing those who had none to assist them.[50] From his birth, he guided the widow[51] and he made her heart sing.[52] Anyone he saw perishing for lack of clothing or needing clothes, he helped.[53]

Job shared his food,[54] and because he opened his door to travelers, no stranger had to spend a night in the street.[55] He was eyes to the blind, feet to the lame, and father to the needy.[56] He put on righteousness as his clothing; justice was his robe and his turban.

---

45. Job 31:29-30: "If I have rejoiced at my enemy's misfortune or gloated over the trouble that came to him—I have not allowed my mouth to sin by invoking a curse against their life . . . ."
46. Job 31:13: "If I have denied justice to any of my servants, whether male or female, when they had a grievance against me . . . ."
47. Job 31:39: "If I have devoured its yield without payment or broken the spirit of its tenants . . . ."
48. Job 31:16: "If I have denied the desires of the poor or let the eyes of the widow grow weary . . . ."
49. Job 31:17-18: "If I have kept my bread to myself, not sharing it with the fatherless—but from my youth I reared them as a father would . . . ."
50. Job 29:12: "Because I rescued the poor who cried for help, and the fatherless who had none to assist them."
51. Job 31:18: "From my birth I guided the widow . . . ."
52. Job 29:13: "The one who was dying blessed me; I made the widow's heart sing."
53. Job 31:19: "If I have seen anyone perishing for lack of clothing, or the needy without garments . . . ."
54. Job 31:31: "If those of my household have never said, 'Who has not been filled with Job's meat?'"
55. Job 31:32: "But no stranger had to spend the night in the street, for my door was always open to the traveler . . . ."
56. Job 29:15-16: "I was eyes to the blind and feet to the lame. I was a father

✿

Some of these claims seem farfetched. Job said he guided the widow from his birth or, as the *King James Version* of the Bible puts it, "from [his] mother's womb."[57] This would mean that even before he was a toddler, Job shared his wisdom with widows. Similarly, he reared the fatherless in his youth. This suggests that before he owned his own home or land, he began raising other people's children.

Like his other claims, Job did not restrict the description of his largesse to one or two people; he spoke globally. Job said he helped "anyone" perishing for lack of clothing or needy without garments. He did not miss a stranger in need.

As those in the giving professions might recognize, Job—amazingly—did not specialize in one or two types of vulnerable populations: He helped them all. The poor. The blind. The lame. The fatherless. The widows. The orphans. And the strangers.

Anyone who has run or witnessed a large food distribution program or charitable organization knows the considerable logistics this would involve. It would require structures to house the operations. It would entail obtaining enormous amounts of food, tirelessly preparing meals, communicating to the villagers the distribution hours, erecting tables, and creating assembly lines to serve the food. It would require finance systems to purchase supplies and pay the workers. It would require clean-up operations, too.

---

to the needy; I took up the case of the stranger."

57. Job 31:18 (KJV): "For from my youth he was brought up with me, as with a father, and I have guided her from my mother's womb . . . ."

For "anyone needing clothes," his servants would have to shear the sheep,[58] sew the clothing, ensure that the sizes were right, and distribute each piece. To be eyes to the blind, Job might have assigned personal assistants to meet their needs. For the lame, he might have instructed couriers to bring food to their homes. To house every traveler, he would need plenty of bedrooms.

Imagine the operations this would require—coupled with boots-on-the-ground intelligence to locate every needy, blind, lame, fatherless, widowed, and traveling person.

Job's representations of his own benevolence raise multiple questions.

First, what happened to his charitable operations after the disasters that took away Job's herds? The servants who died in the disasters were tending the animals. Where were those running Job's feeding, clothing, and housing programs? In contrast to the feeding programs of the Biblical Patriarch Joseph,[59] for which the source and method of storing food was described, the Bible contains no references to how Job's massive operations were organized or how they were dismantled when disaster struck.

---

58. Job 31:19-20: "If I have seen anyone perishing for lack of clothing, or the needy without garments, and their hearts did not bless me . . . for warming them with the fleece from my sheep . . . ."

59. Genesis 41:47-49: "During the seven years of abundance the land produced plentifully. Joseph collected all the food produced in those seven years of abundance in Egypt and stored it in the cities. In each city he put the food grown in the fields surrounding it. Joseph stored up huge quantities of grain, like the sand of the sea; it was so much that he stopped keeping records because it was beyond measure."

Second, after the disasters, why didn't Job express concern about the people he could no longer help? People who manage charitable operations connect emotionally to those involved. They know their names. They know their stories. They know their families. Such a massive operation would have been Job's "baby," something he invested in since . . . well, from the time he was born. And when the operations suddenly shut down, one would expect that he would have worried about the fates of those he no longer served. Why did he not lament the loss of his mission—that he could no longer be used by God to serve these suffering people?

In contrast, the Apostle Paul, amidst his suffering and impending death, spent his time in prison fixated on what would happen to those entrusted to his care. With great passion for others, not for himself, Paul guided the churches and gave instructions on everything from putting on the armor of God to staying in prayer at all times.[60]

Corrie ten Boom, the Dutch woman who lost her family to the horrors of Nazi Germany, worried continuously about the souls and fates of the inmates who suffered with her in the horrific conditions of the concentration camps. She was gripped also with concern about the Jewish refugees hidden in her home when the Nazis invaded it.[61]

---

60. Ephesians 6:11-12: "Put on the full armor of God, so that you can take your stand against the devil's schemes. For our struggle is not against flesh and blood, but against the rulers, against the authorities, against the powers of this dark world and against the spiritual forces of evil in the heavenly realms."
61. Corrie ten Boom, *The Hiding Place*, (Grand Rapids, Michigan, Chosen Books), 25th Anniversary Edition, 143.

Yet Job, in all his laments, never once expressed concern for the welfare of those he had been blessed to have helped.

Third, and most telling of all, why did not one of the vast numbers of people he helped appreciate him enough to send a note of condolence or bring a dish of stew when he faced his own suffering? Why didn't they rally around him? Except for four friends, who vigorously challenged his claims of blamelessness, and his wife, who encouraged him to die, Job was universally deserted. As we shall learn, not one person took his claims of benevolence at face value.

Job's claims of righteousness have a familiar ring. In Luke 18:9-14, Jesus tells the parable of the Pharisee and the Tax Collector, as follows:

> *To some who were confident of their own righteousness and looked down on everyone else, Jesus told this parable: "Two men went up to the temple to pray, one a Pharisee and the other a tax collector. The Pharisee stood by himself and prayed: 'God, I thank you that I am not like other people—robbers, evildoers, adulterers—or even like this tax collector. I fast twice a week and give a tenth of all I get.' But the tax collector stood at a distance. He would not even look up to heaven, but beat his breast and said, 'God, have mercy on me, a sinner.' I tell you that this man, rather than the other, went home justified before God. For all those who exalt themselves will be humbled, and those who humble themselves will be exalted."*

It is difficult to conceive that any humble, God-fearing man or woman could believe that he or she has done everything right. Every time we step out of the flow of the Spirit, every stray word of gossip we utter, every time we withhold forgiveness, every proud thought we think, every time we act unkindly, and whenever we walk in fear, anxiety, or despair instead of faith, we fail to meet the standards of righteousness.

Galatians 6:3 states, "If anyone thinks they are something when they are not, they deceive themselves." 1 John 1:8 says, "If we claim to be without sin, we deceive ourselves and the truth is not in us." Proverbs 20:9 states, "Who can say, 'I have kept my heart pure. I am clean and without sin'?"

Like King David, who was blinded to his sin with Bathsheba until Nathan the Prophet helped remove the veil,[62] evidence suggests that Job saw his world through spiritual blinders.

---

62. 2 Samuel 12:1-7: "The Lord sent Nathan to David. When he came to him, he said, 'There were two men in a certain town, one rich and the other poor. The rich man had a very large number of sheep and cattle, but the poor man had nothing except one little ewe lamb he had bought. He raised it, and it grew up with him and his children. It shared his food, drank from his cup and even slept in his arms. It was like a daughter to him. Now a traveler came to the rich man, but the rich man refrained from taking one of his own sheep or cattle to prepare a meal for the traveler who had come to him. Instead, he took the ewe lamb that belonged to the poor man and prepared it for the one who had come to him.' David burned with anger against the man and said to Nathan, 'As surely as the Lord lives, the man who did this must die! He must pay for that lamb four times over, because he did such a thing and had no pity.' Then Nathan said to David, 'You are the man!'" In his subsequent confession of sin in Psalm 51:5, King David said, "Surely I was sinful at birth, sinful from the time my mother conceived me." Compare that confession to Job's belief that he guided widows from his birth.

Job was gripped by a powerful delusion about himself, others, and God.

As Job's friend Bildad asked, "How then can a mortal be righteous before God? How can one born of woman be pure?"[63] Bildad was right. When Job professed to be pure and universally benevolent, he was claiming the impossible. As William Gurnall states in his book, *The Christian in Complete Armour*, "Hypocrisy is the loudest lie, because it is given to God himself."[64]

---

63. Job 25:4.
64. Gurnall, *The Christian in Complete Armour*. The reprint does not provide page numbers.

Chapter 3

FAMILY AND FRIENDS

"You demanded security from
your relatives for no reason."

—ELIPHAZ TO JOB
Job 22:6

W hen King David lost his son Absalom, he could not be consoled.

The king covered his face and cried aloud, "O
my son Absalom! O Absalom, my son, my son!"[65]

When the Biblical Patriarch Jacob believed that a ferocious animal killed his son Joseph, he tore his clothes, put on sackcloth, and mourned many days.

All his sons and daughters came to comfort him, but
he refused to be comforted. "No," he said, "I will
continue to mourn until I join my son in the grave."
So his father wept for him.[66]

When the Apostle Peter visited the mourning party for Dorcas, "all the widows stood around him, crying and showing him the robes and other clothing that Dorcas had made while she was still with them."[67]

---

65. 2 Samuel 19:4.
66. Genesis 37:34-35.
67. Acts 9:39.

Gathering with friends and recalling the lives of departed loved ones are natural parts of grieving. But while Job faced the unimaginable tragedy of losing ten children, curiously, in 42 chapters, Job mentions his departed children twice—and then only in passing.

> *Oh, for the days when . . . the Almighty was still with me and my children were around me.*[68]
> *Surely, God, you have worn me out; you have devastated my entire household.*[69]

In fact, Job never mentions the names of his dead children—not even once. Nor does he recall their deeds or invoke their memories. Why? Was Job so grief-stricken that he was unable to articulate his feelings? Did numbness and shock close his mouth?

Job may have focused silently on the death of his children during the seven days of mourning[70] in which he and three friends, Eliphaz, Bildad, and Zophar, sat without words. But after that, Job talked extensively—so much so that his friends and even the Lord commented on his many words. Job's focus, however, was not on his children. He admitted as much when he explained that a person who loses hope focuses not on his offspring, but on himself. "They feel but the pain of their own bodies and mourn only for themselves," he said.[71]

---

68. Job 29:4-5: "Oh, for the days when I was in my prime, when God's intimate friendship blessed my house, when the Almighty was still with me and my children were around me."
69. Job 16:7.
70. Job 2:13: "Then they sat on the ground with him for seven days and seven nights. No one said a word to him, because they saw how great his suffering was." Elihu apparently was not with the three friends. He is mentioned later.
71. Job 14:21-22: "If their children are honored, they do not know it; if their

Job was fixated on his own innocence, God's injustice, and the other type of grief that gripped him most intensely: his loss of reputation.

Why, then, wasn't the loss of his children at the forefront of his mind? And what kind of person mourns the loss of stature over the loss of his children? Perhaps something else was going on.

Our primary knowledge of Job's ten children is that they feasted often, eating and drinking wine, particularly on their birthdays.[72] Their periods of feasting were frequent enough that it became a "regular custom" for Job to arrange for ceremonial purification and to offer burnt offerings for them in case they sinned and cursed God in their hearts.[73] Cursing God was considered blasphemy and the penalty for such a sin was death, under Old Testament regulations.[74] Although many scholars believe that Job was Arabian and that these regulations were formally issued after he lived, Job was clearly aware of the prohibition because he refused to engage in it when his

---

offspring are brought low, they do not see it. They feel but the pain of their own bodies and mourn only for themselves."

72. Job 1:4: "His sons used to hold feasts in their homes on their birthdays, and they would invite their three sisters to eat and drink with them." The word "wine" is added in Job 1:18.

73. Job 1:5: "When a period of feasting had run its course, Job would make arrangements for them to be purified. Early in the morning he would sacrifice a burnt offering for each of them, thinking, 'Perhaps my children have sinned and cursed God in their hearts.' This was Job's regular custom."

74. Leviticus 24:15-16: "Say to the Israelites: 'Anyone who curses their God will be held responsible; anyone who blasphemes the name of the Lord is to be put to death.'"

ungodly wife urged him to do it.[75] In the New Testament, blasphemy against the Spirit could never be forgiven.[76] It was considered a sin worthy of eternal damnation.

Bildad told Job that his children had sinned and that, in permitting them to die, God gave them over to the penalty of their sin.[77] Such a suggestion to a grieving father would be cruel and thoughtless under any circumstance, but to accuse them without evidence would be unconscionable. Why Bildad made such an uncompassionate statement is not explained, but Job's ceremonial actions suggest that his children were not righteously devoted to God. For what righteous child would consider cursing God? It would be like praying every night that your son or daughter does not rob a bank. If he or she has no proclivity for robbing banks, such a prayer would be absurd.

The probable scenario is that Job's children, showered with wealth and growing up in the shadow of their powerful father, lived a superficial life, focused on partying accompanied by other sins. While one would expect that children growing up in the home of the greatest philanthropist of the East would follow their father's example and help with his charitable operations, there is no record that they did so.

---

75. Job 2:9-10: "His wife said to him, 'Are you still maintaining your integrity? Curse God and die!' He replied, 'You are talking like a foolish woman. Shall we accept good from God, and not trouble?' In all this, Job did not sin in what he said."

76. Matthew 12:31: "And so I tell you, every kind of sin and slander can be forgiven, but blasphemy against the Spirit will not be forgiven." Mark 3:29: "But whoever blasphemes against the Holy Spirit will never be forgiven; they are guilty of an eternal sin."

77. Job 8:4: "When your children sinned against him, he gave them over to the penalty of their sin."

Proverbs 3:12 states that a father who delights in his son disciplines him, but the Bible does not report that Job encouraged his children to live more godly, sober lives, or that he intervened and pleaded with them to avoid cursing God in their hearts. Instead, it appears that he stayed away from their frequent parties and resorted to ceremonial rituals time after time to ensure that they were "covered," from a religious point of view. In reality, the Lord did not want sacrifices if they had not turned away from sin.[78]

While Job may have been distant from his first set of children, his other familial relationships were weak as well. While one would presume that most wives would want their husbands to live, Job's wife urged him to die, a fate reserved for the wicked, whose widows do not weep for them.[79] By urging her husband to curse God, Job's wife was willing to see him face eternal consequences. Job mourned that, in his illness, his breath was offensive to her, something that a devoted caregiving spouse would deem inconsequential.

Job blamed God for alienating him from his family. In fact, he was "loathsome" to them; his relatives had abandoned him. His friends were no better. Not only were they estranged from him, they detested him. Even the few friends who sat with him were "miserable comforters."[80]

Job summed it up this way:

---

78. Isaiah 1:12-13 (TLB): "Who wants your sacrifices when you have no sorrow for your sins?"

79. Job 27:13, 15: "Here is the fate God allots to the wicked . . . and their widows will not weep for them."

80. Job 16:2: "You are miserable comforters, all of you!"

*He has alienated my family from me; my acquain-
tances are completely estranged from me. My relatives
have gone away; my closest friends have forgotten
me. . . . My breath is offensive to my wife; I am loathsome to my own family. . . . All my intimate friends
detest me; those I love have turned against me.*[81]

This reaction to the suffering of a good person defies logic.

When a generous person suffers catastrophe, many
surround him with support. They bring food. They grieve.
They run errands. They organize fund-raising drives. They
bring messages of love and cheer. They turn out at funerals by
the hundreds. When a man who has blessed untold numbers
with his largesse—as Job represented he did—one would
anticipate an even greater show of affection. Night-time vigils.
Constant streams of well-wishers. Warm hugs.

While hospitality was considered a virtue in the ancient
Middle Eastern culture, Job did not benefit from it after his
loss of wealth. Instead, in a peculiar response to the suffering
of a benevolent man, the "mockers" came out in full force.
Although holy men of God have been mocked throughout the
centuries, it is because they spoke uncomfortable truths against
obstinate people. But this was not the case with Job because,
by his own account, all spoke well of him before his downfall.

So who would walk away from a man who has been generous
to orphans and widows? Why would intimate friends detest
him? Why would his family abandon him in his greatest time
of need? Who would spit in the face of a suffering man who

---

81. Job 19:13-19.

lived a generous life? More importantly, *why* would they go out of their way to scorn such a kind man? It takes passion, energy, time, and focus to muster up such ridicule.

And it takes *motive*.

Was every single one of the hundreds—perhaps thousands—of beneficiaries of Job's past wealth and wisdom so cold-hearted that they thought his suffering merited ridicule?

The answer lies in a provocative theory: Perhaps Job wasn't the loving and honorable brother, relative, friend, and civic leader he imagined himself to be. In fact, in one of the book's explosive throwaway lines, his friend Eliphaz makes serious and startling accusations about how Job treated his relatives. Eliphaz said:

> *You demanded security from your relatives for no reason.*[82]

Security is what a debtor pledges when he makes a loan agreement. If the borrower does not, or cannot, pay what he owes, the lender is permitted to take possession of whatever asset the debtor pledged as security. Take, for example, the American mortgage crisis that began in 2008. Nearly ten million families lost their homes to foreclosure during that crisis.[83] In the Bible, security was taken in the form of fields, vineyards, and homes—even children.[84] Taking security from

---

82. Job 22:6.
83. Badger, Emily, "How the housing crisis left us more racially segregated," *Washington Post Wonkblog*, May 8, 2015.
84. Nehemiah 5:3: "Others were saying, 'We are mortgaging our fields, our vineyards and our homes to get grain during the famine.'" Job 24:9: "The fatherless child is snatched from the breast; the infant of the poor is seized for a debt."

those who were desperately poor was considered wrong. In Deuteronomy 24:6, accepting a pair of millstones as security for a debt was prohibited because doing so would take away a person's livelihood and food. Taking a widow's garment as security was also forbidden.[85] In Exodus 22:26, a lender who took a neighbor's cloak as security for a loan was required to return it before sunset.

Although Biblical scholars believe that these prohibitions were issued after Job's trials occurred, Job was doubtlessly aware of the ethics surrounding the practice of taking security from the impoverished. In Job 24, he criticized those who took the widow's ox as a pledge[86] and those who seized the infant of the poor as security for an unpaid debt.[87]

In accusing Job of taking security from his relatives for no reason, Eliphaz challenged Job as being guilty of the very thing he accused others of doing. Eliphaz portrayed Job as a wealthy but ruthless lender who placed money above concern for his own family.

Eliphaz made other serious and startling accusations about how Job conducted his affairs. Like the New Testament Pharisees, who made lengthy public prayers for a show but devoured widows' houses,[88] Job sent the widows away empty-

---

85. Deuteronomy 24:17: "Do not deprive the foreigner or the fatherless of justice, or take the cloak of the widow as a pledge."
86. Job 24:3: "They drive away the orphan's donkey and take the widow's ox in pledge."
87. Job 24:9: "The fatherless child is snatched from the breast; the infant of the poor is seized for a debt."
88. Mark 12:38-40: "As he taught, Jesus said, 'Watch out for the teachers of the law. They like to walk around in flowing robes and be greeted with respect in the marketplaces, and have the most important seats in the

handed, according to Eliphaz. Job stripped people of their clothing. He withheld food from the hungry. Indeed, Eliphaz challenged the very heart of Job's representations that he was a generous man when he said:

> You stripped people of their clothing, leaving them naked. You gave no water to the weary and you withheld food from the hungry, though you were a powerful man, owning land—an honored man, living on it. And you sent widows away empty-handed and broke the strength of the fatherless.[89]

Elihu, too, was concerned about Job's business practices. He warned Job not to try to get out of his situation by taking a large bribe or longing for the night to drag people away from their homes.[90] Such statements would not be logical or warranted unless Job was predisposed to these types of behaviors. Elihu's warning suggests that Job took security—repossessed homes—at night to hide his actions.

Continuing his argument, Elihu warned Job to turn back from evil, which he "seem[ed] to prefer to affliction." This statement suggests that Job was prone to finding nefarious man-made ways to escape from the suffering that was

synagogues and the places of honor at banquets. They devour widows' houses and for a show make lengthy prayers. These men will be punished most severely.'"

89. Job 22:6-9.

90. Job 36:17-20: "But now you are laden with the judgment due the wicked; judgment and justice have taken hold of you. Be careful that no one entices you by riches; do not let a large bribe turn you aside. Would your wealth or even all your mighty efforts sustain you so you would not be in distress? Do not long for the night, to drag people away from their homes."

intended to teach him.[91] Elihu made other allegations against Job. He accused Job of associating with evildoers.[92] When the other friends challenged Job, Elihu described Job's answers to them as wicked.[93] Furthermore, Elihu became angry at Job "because Job refused to admit that he had sinned and that God was right in punishing him."[94]

When indirect statements are considered, the evidence against Job mounts. Job's friends frequently referred to mythical third parties with the same attributes or fates as Job to make a point. Job took these references personally, acknowledging that his friends were talking about him.

For example, Eliphaz described the wicked who loved bribes[95] and suffered the same fate as Job. Although Eliphaz' words did not mention Job, Job fully understood that the mythical wicked man was, in fact, he. "I could make fine speeches against you and shake my head at you," Job responded.[96] While an innocent person would normally be aghast at such accusations and immediately deny that he committed such crimes, Job instead turned the tables and accused the accuser.

Aligning with Elihu's allegations, Zophar talked about a

---

91. Job 36:21-22: "Beware of turning to evil, which you seem to prefer to affliction. God is exalted in his power. Who is a teacher like him?" The Living Bible begins the verse with "Turn back from evil . . . ."
92. Job 34:8: "He keeps company with evildoers; he associates with the wicked."
93. Job 34:36: "Oh, that Job might be tested to the utmost for answering like a wicked man!"
94. Job 32:2 (NLT).
95. Job 15:34: "For the company of the godless will be barren, and fire will consume the tents of those who love bribes."
96. Job 16:4.

wicked man who suffered the same fate as Job because he "oppressed the poor and left them destitute; he has seized houses he did not build."[97] Job responded by challenging Zophar to "mock on," but only after allowing Job to speak.[98] Job told his accusers that if they were right, his sin was none of their business.[99]

Bildad described a wicked man whose own schemes took him down.[100] Although Bildad did not refer to Job when he described the wicked man, Job recognized that Bildad was talking about him. "Ten times now you have reproached me," he responded to Bildad. "Shamelessly you attack me."[101]

Elihu concurred in describing the wicked who "caused the cry of the poor to come before [God] so that He heard the cry of the needy."[102] This indirect statement correlates to Elihu's direct statements about Job.

When one removes the metaview of Job's righteousness and what has been a bewildering story for generations, a much different picture begins to emerge. If Job were ruthless, arrogant, and hypocritical, as his friends alleged, the ridicule he received would make sense. His contemptuous business practices would explain why the villagers universally cheered

---

97. Job 20:19.
98. Job 21:3: "Bear with me while I speak, and after I have spoken, mock on."
99. Job 19:4: "If it is true that I have gone astray, my error remains my concern alone."
100. Job 18:7: "The vigor of his step is weakened; his own schemes throw him down."
101. Job 19:3.
102. Job 34:28

at the fall of this powerful man. It would explain the mass exodus of family and friends. It would explain the harsh reprimands of his four friends, who desperately sought Job's repentance and restoration. It would explain Job's lack of concern for the recipients of his alleged benevolence and even for his own children. It would explain the Lord's powerful rebuke of Job in Chapters 38 to 41. It would explain why, in James 5:11, the Lord was described as full of "compassion and mercy" in his dealings with Job.[103]

And it might explain the Lord's long silence before answering Job. Elihu told Job, "He does not answer when men cry out because of the arrogance of the wicked."[104] Isaiah 59:2 states, "But your iniquities have separated you from your God; your sins have hidden His face from you, so that He will not hear." The Lord did not answer Job until he became quiet and ready to listen.

Suddenly, the book of Job makes sense.

Those who have walked the halls of power recognize the archetypal character suggested by Job's self-described perfection. Humble leaders understand that their power is fleeting, but those inflated with pride are unable to see the world—or their place in it—with sober clarity. Like all of us, they have blind spots to their own weaknesses, but their

---

103. James 5:11: "You have heard of Job's perseverance and have seen what the Lord finally brought about. The Lord is full of compassion and mercy."
104. Job 35:12-15: "He does not answer when people cry out because of the arrogance of the wicked. Indeed, God does not listen to their empty plea; the Almighty pays no attention to it. How much less, then, will He listen when you say that you do not see Him, that your case is before Him and you must wait for Him and further, that His anger never punishes and He does not take the least notice of wickedness."

delusion becomes extreme. Proud and aggressive, they do not tolerate being challenged. They ruthlessly suppress dissent. They demand absolute loyalty—as did Job, who, incredibly, accused his friends of "wickedly" taking God's side over his[105] and insisted that his friends be loyal even if he abandoned the fear of the Almighty.[106] Narcissistic, they surround themselves with sycophants who use flattery for their own advantage,[107] providing the leader with the universal, but illusory, commendation he craves. "How smart you are," "how good you are," or "how powerful you are," members of the inner circle say to gain a piece of the largesse. But once the largesse disappears—often in a moment of disaster foreseen by everyone except the leader—so do they.

Insecure leaders are obsessed with how they are viewed in the world. "The hypocrite is nobody, except on the stage," writes William Gurnall in *The Christian in Complete Armour*. "He courts the world for its applause."[108] To their detriment, they bask in false compliments[109] and see no risk. Their followers are driven by self-interest or fear, but not respect or love. Perhaps subconsciously, Job recognized this phenomenon when he spoke of the wicked and said, "No one criticizes them openly."[110]

---

105. Job 13:7-8: "Will you speak wickedly on God's behalf? Will you speak deceitfully for Him? Will you show Him partiality? Will you argue the case for God?"

106. Job 6:14-15 (CSB): "A despairing man should receive loyalty from his friends, even if he abandons the fear of the Almighty. My brothers are as treacherous as a wadi, as seasonal streams that overflow."

107. Jude 1:16: "These people . . . flatter others for their own advantage."

108. Gurnall, *The Christian in Complete Armour*. The reprint does not provide page numbers.

109. Proverbs 26:28: "A lying tongue hates those it hurts, and a flattering mouth works ruin."

110. Job 21:31 (NLT): "No one criticizes them openly or pays them back for what they have done."

Job, of course, insisted that this was not he. Throughout the Biblical book in his name, Job protested his innocence. Early on, he accused his friends of smearing him with lies.[111] After that, his friends' allegations became more intense, but Job told them, "I will defend my integrity until I die."[112] Eventually his friends gave up, concluding that they could not convince him. They stopped talking when they realized the extent to which Job was righteous "in his own eyes."[113]

Who, then, was lying? Job, or Eliphaz, Bildad, and Zophar, followed by Elihu, who spoke later?

A traditional view is that Job's first three friends cruelly, wrongly, and judgmentally ascribed sin to him because they believed that God would not have punished Job if he were innocent. Proof of the friends' misguided thinking was that God reprimanded them for their folly.

However, this interpretation does not ring true. Why?

First, a closer look at the reprimand illustrates that it was not issued for speaking wrongly about Job, but about God.

> *After the Lord had said these things to Job, he said to Eliphaz the Temanite, "I am angry with you and your two friends, because you have not spoken the truth **about Me**."*[114]

---

111. Job 13:4: "You, however, smear me with lies; you are worthless physicians, all of you!"
112. Job 27:5 (NLT): "I will never concede that you are right; I will defend my integrity until I die."
113. Job 32:1: "So these three men stopped answering Job, because he was righteous in his own eyes." See also Proverbs 26:12.
114. Job 42:7: Emphasis added by author.

Second, although Elihu was unhappy at how Job's other friends presented their arguments, he wholeheartedly agreed with their character assessment. If the Lord reprimanded the first three friends because they erred in their assessment of Job's character, Elihu would have been rebuked as well.

Third, if the friends were wrong and Job was right, Job would not have eventually repented and taken back everything he said.[115]

Fourth, God angrily accused Job of talking with "words without knowledge"[116] and commended him only after he repented.

Fifth, it was no coincidence that four witnesses, not one, challenged Job. Deuteronomy 19:15 states, "One witness is not enough to convict anyone accused of any crime or offense they may have committed. A matter must be established by the testimony of two or three witnesses."

Sixth, the friends' allegations were not cloaked in caveats or generalized speculation. If they were merely speculating that Job must have done *something* wrong, they would have left the allegations vague. Job's friends didn't accuse him of sexual immorality, worshipping idols, or gossiping. All four charged him with the same sin: engaging in devastating business practices that took advantage of the vulnerable. Eliphaz' accusations about Job's mistreatment of his relatives, the widows, and the fatherless were presented as

---

115. Job 42:6 (NLT): "I take back everything I said, and I sit in dust and ashes to show my repentance."
116. Job 38:2: "Who is this that obscures My plans with words without knowledge?"

cold, hard facts.[117] Given the massive charitable operations Job would have needed to support his claims of benevolence, these allegations, if false, would have been easy for him to counter.

Seventh, while falsely accusing Job in his immense grief would have been beyond wicked—sociopathic, even—there is no evidence that his friends possessed such evil character. When the friends came to visit him, they wept when they saw how much he was suffering, and they sat in silence for seven days out of respect for his sorrow.[118] Although they were blunt-speaking, likely reflecting a culture where directness was prized, they repeatedly urged Job to repent so that he would be restored, a sign that they wished him well. Furthermore, if his friends were simply self-righteous and judgmental, they would have acted as if they themselves were without sin. Instead, they insisted that no one could make that claim. In humility, Bildad said, "For we were born only yesterday and know nothing."[119]

Eliphaz claimed that a spirit spoke to him in a dream.[120] The message was consistent with what God has spoken

---

117. One Bible translation, the *New Living Translation*, inserts the subjunctive mood in Job 22:6, speculating that the mistreatment "must have" occurred, but other translations use the past tense, stating that it did occur.

118. Job 2:12-13: "When they saw him from a distance, they could hardly recognize him; they began to weep aloud, and they tore their robes and sprinkled dust on their heads. Then they sat on the ground with him for seven days and seven nights. No one said a word to him because they saw how great his suffering was."

119. Job 8:9.

120. Job 4:15-17: "A spirit glided past my face, and the hair on my body stood on end. It stopped, but I could not tell what it was. A form stood before my eyes, and I heard a hushed voice: 'Can a mortal be more righteous than God? Can even a strong man be more pure than his Maker?'"

throughout the ages: man is not pure. This suggests that Eliphaz was listening to the right spirit—a spirit sent from God. Furthermore, names in that age were given to reflect a man's character and the name Eliphaz, according to many scholars, means "Pure Gold."

Job's friends spent weeks—perhaps months[121]—away from their homes to comfort Job. What would they gain by such selfless sacrifice, if not to try to bring a suffering man to self-realization and forgiveness? What would motivate them to concoct tales of Job's wickedness during a time when differences are normally set aside to bring comfort to the suffering? And what is the likelihood that all four would be in universal agreement that Job engaged in wicked business practices? Wouldn't one of them come to Job's defense if the allegations about abusing the vulnerable were false? These men were not shy about sharing their opinions.

Finally, if Job's four friends were evil-hearted, so was every other person in his life. The others either abandoned him or mocked him, suggesting they were either cold-hearted and ungrateful or they saw Job for who he was. The former theory is dispelled by what eventually happened: They came around. "All his brothers and sisters and everyone who had known him before came and ate with him in his house. They comforted and consoled him over all the trouble the Lord had brought on him, and each one gave him a piece of silver and a gold ring."[122]

Why did they wait months to come? What changed?

---

121. Job 7:3: "So I have been allotted months of futility . . . ."
122. Job 42:11.

Evidence suggests that family and community healing came about because of a momentous event: Job made an earth-shattering confession. Despite his prominence in the religious community, his self-proclaimed righteousness, and his decades of performing religious rituals, Job admitted that he never actually knew God. In a powerful one-line statement, Job confessed that his knowledge of God was based on hearsay. He told the Lord, "I had only heard about You before . . . ."[123]

Although it required tremendous suffering and a confrontation with God using the most powerful representations of nature as evidence of His care for the earth,[124] the Lord broke through Job's blinders. Job confessed that he had spoken about things he did not understand,[125] and he repented in dust and ashes.[126]

In his book, *Not in God's Name, Confronting Religious Violence*, Rabbi Jonathan Sacks chronicles the rivalries of Old Testament siblings. Rabbi Sacks demonstrates that the Lord's pressing desire is that warring siblings be reconciled—and this was achieved through the healing of broken relationships between Isaac and Ishmael, Jacob and Esau, and Joseph and his brothers,[127] typically after role reversals. One way we

---

123. Job 42:5 (NLT): "I had only heard about You before, but now I have seen You with my own eyes."
124. Job, Chapter 38.
125. Job 42:3: "You asked, 'Who is this that obscures My plans without knowledge?' Surely I spoke of things I did not understand, things too wonderful for me to know."
126. Job 42:6: "Therefore I despise myself and repent in dust and ashes."
127. Sacks, Jonathan. *Not in God's Name: Confronting Religious Violence.* (New York, Schoken Books, a division of Penguin Random House LLC., 2015), 156.

learn not to commit evil is to experience an event from the perspective of the victim, states Rabbi Sacks.[128]

To the stories of Old Testament leaders re-unified with their siblings can be added the drama of Job, who was reconciled to the family members he estranged by taking financial advantage of them.

Following his repentance, the Lord blessed Job with a second family, giving him seven sons and three daughters. While the author omits the names of Job's sons, he demonstrates that Job showed particular fondness for his daughters, giving them names of deep affection: Jemimah, Keziah, and Keren-happuch,[129] that is, "Little Dove," "Sweet-Scented Spice," and "Horn of Antimony." Job—the man who had devastated widows—now ensured that his daughters would receive an inheritance.[130]

Why does the author of the Book of Job give special attention to Job's daughters? Because esteeming women is a sign of a man in relationship with God. The prayers of husbands who are not considerate of their wives are hindered, the Apostle Peter states.[131] Christ, by bringing women into his inner circle, showed women an unusual level of respect

---

128. Ibid, 158.
129. Job 42:13-14: "And he also had seven sons and three daughters. The first daughter he named Jemimah, the second Keziah and the third Keren-Happuch."
130. Job 42:15: "Nowhere in all the land were there found women as beautiful as Job's daughters, and their father granted them an inheritance along with their brothers."
131. I Peter 3:7: "Husbands, in the same way be considerate as you live with your wives, and treat them with respect as the weaker partner and as heirs with you of the gracious gift of life, so that nothing will hinder your prayers."

for His day. The Old Testament prophet Joel predicted that daughters would be among those who would one day receive the Spirit and prophesy.[132]

After this, Job lived a hundred and forty years; he saw his children and their children to the fourth generation. And so Job died, an old man and full of years.[133]

---

132. Joel 2:28-29: "And afterward, I will pour out my Spirit on all people. Your sons and daughters will prophesy, your old men will dream dreams, your young men will see visions. Even on my servants, both men and women, I will pour out my Spirit in those days."
133. Job 42:16-17.

Chapter 4

SERVANTS

"Of what use was the strength of their hands to me,
since their vigor had gone from them?"

—JOB OF THE YOUTH WHO LIVED AMONG THE ROCKS
Job 30:2

I n communications of catastrophic news of death and
destruction, the normal order of information begins with the
loss of lives. Reports of property damage follow. But when
Job was told of the calamities that befell him, the news of each
was delivered in an unexpected sequence. The loss of animals
was communicated to him before the loss of human life.

A messenger came to Job and said, "The oxen were
plowing and the donkeys were grazing nearby, and
the Sabeans attacked and made off with them.
They put the servants to the sword, and I am the only
one who has escaped to tell you!"

While he was still speaking, another messenger came
and said, "The fire of God fell from the heavens and
burned up the sheep *and the servants, and I am the*
only one who has escaped to tell you!"

While he was still speaking, another messenger came
and said, "The Chaldeans formed three raiding parties
and swept down on your camels and made off

*with them. They put the servants to the sword, and I
am the only one who has escaped to tell you!*"[134]

In communicating the catastrophic events, the messengers
may have saved the worst news until last to soften the
blow. Or, perhaps they knew their master well enough to
understand where his priorities lay. They may have known
that Job would want to hear about his herds first, and that he,
like other powerful businessmen throughout the ages, viewed
his servants as dispensable.

Job's servants were among those who abandoned him
completely in his suffering.

> *My guests and my female servants count me a
> foreigner; they look on me as on a stranger. I summon
> my servant, but he does not answer, though I beg him
> with my own mouth.*[135]

Although Job claimed to have treated his servants fairly,
not one of them came to help him in his distress. This is
an unexpected reaction from those who presumably served
Job daily in his home for years and would have found his
egalitarian[136] view toward them extraordinarily unusual and
kind. In a time when slaves were treated cruelly, branded on
the soles of their feet,[137] Job's benevolence to his servants would

---

134. Job 1:13-19. Emphasis added by author.
135. Job 19:15-16.
136. Job 31:13-15: "If I have denied justice to any of my servants, whether
male or female, when they had a grievance against me, what will I do
when God confronts me? What will I answer when called to account? Did
not He who made me in the womb make them? Did not the same one
form us both within our mothers?"
137. Job 13:27: "You fasten my feet in shackles; you keep close watch on all
my paths by putting marks on the soles of my feet."

have been a glorious but startling contrast to the suffering lives of others in the same predicament. The normal reaction, then, would be to run to the aid of such an unusually kind man.

A throwaway line suggests the reason why they stayed away: Job's actions did not measure up to his claims. In reality, Job evaluated his servants, or potential servants, from a cold and mercenary point of view:

> *Of what use was the strength of their hands to me,*
> *since their vigor had gone from them?*[138]

Job had a curious relationship with a group of young men who lived among the rocks, on dry streambeds, and in holes in the ground.[139] It was their strength that Job evaluated and found wanting. They were too weak from hunger to be of use to him. Job eyed not only these young men as potential servants—only to find them inadequate—he evaluated their fathers and found them equally unworthy of working for him. Job said he would have disdained to put their fathers with his sheep dogs.[140]

Apparently, Job's massive feeding programs for the poor missed this group:

> *Haggard from want and hunger, they roamed the*
> *parched land in desolate wastelands at night. In the*
> *brush they gathered salt herbs, and their food was*
> *the root of the broom bush.*[141]

---

138. Job 30:2.
139. Job 30:6: "They were forced to live in the dry stream beds, among the rocks and in holes in the ground."
140. Job 30:1: "But now they mock me, men younger than I, whose fathers I would have disdained to put with my sheep dogs."
141. Job 30:3-4.

These youths were hopelessly poor, banished from human society, driven from the land, and shouted at as if they were thieves. They huddled from the cold in the undergrowth of the bushes.[142]

The young men detested Job,[143] the man whose entire life—by his own account—revolved around feeding the poor and serving the vulnerable. Once God unstrung the bow and afflicted Job, these young men threw off restraint and spit in Job's face,[144] mocked him, and used songs to do it.[145]

Compare their response to that of the orphan boys who revered Theodore Roosevelt, Sr., in gratitude for the philanthropy and love he showed them. The elder Roosevelt, father of United States President Theodore Roosevelt, visited the orphaned children at the Newsboys' Lodging House in New York. According to Paul Grondahl, author of *I Rose Like a Rocket: The Political Education of Theodore Roosevelt*, the elder Roosevelt's work in the Lodging House "seemed to attract and win the sympathies of every boy in the house. He knew them by name, he knew their histories, and, whenever he came there, they would gather round him, and [he] would

---

142. Job 30:5-8: "They were banished from human society, shouted at as if they were thieves. They were forced to live in the dry stream beds, among the rocks and in holes in the ground. They brayed among the bushes and huddled in the undergrowth. A base and nameless brood, they were driven out of the land."

143. Perhaps Proverbs 28:11 applies to such an unhappy relationship: "The rich are wise in their own eyes; one who is poor and discerning sees how deluded they are."

144. Job 30:10: "They detest me and keep their distance; they do not hesitate to spit in my face."

145. Job 30:9: "And now those young men mock me in song; I have become a byword among them."

question each one as to what he was doing, and give him advice and sympathy and directions . . . . Undoubtedly the great impelling power of his life was a sense of duty, essentially implanted by his Christian belief."[146]

While it is possible that the hungry youths who mocked Job had received food, clothing, and kindness from the wealthy man but were ungrateful for his benevolence, Job's comments suggest the opposite: He disdained them and they hated him for it. Because they were hungry and they, without exception, hated Job, there is no indication that Job tried to relieve their suffering.[147] Rather, Job opined that their intense hunger made these youths weak and unfit to work for him. For a man who claimed to help such vulnerable populations, his attitude presents a startling insight into the true condition of his soul.

In the New Testament, the Apostle Paul reminded his followers that Christ made himself "of no reputation" by taking on the very nature of a servant[148] and that his followers were to have the mind of Christ,[149] but this servant-like

---

146. Paul Grondahl, *I Rose Like a Rocket: The Political Education of Theodore Roosevelt*, (Lincoln, Nebraska. University of Nebraska Press, Originally Published by Free Press, a Division of Simon & Schuster, Inc., 2004), 5.

147. Job 22:8-9: Eliphaz told Job, "Though you were a powerful man, owning land—an honored man, living on it. And you sent widows away empty-handed and broke the strength of the fatherless." Although Eliphaz spoke in the past tense about Job's ownership of land, there is no record that the tragedies took away the property that Job owned.

148. Philippians 2:7 (KJV): "But [Christ Jesus] made himself of no reputation, and took upon him the form of a servant, and was made in the likeness of men."

149. 1 Corinthians 2:16: "For who hath known the mind of the Lord, that He may instruct him? But we have the mind of Christ."

attitude appeared to be foreign to Job. It was likely Job's attitude to his own servants that colored his view of God.

> *Do not mortals have hard service on earth? Are not their days like those of hired laborers? Like a slave longing for the evening shadows, or a hired laborer waiting to be paid, so I have been allotted months of futility, and nights of misery have been assigned to me.*[150]

As we shall see in the next chapter, Job, now reduced to the role of servant, viewed God as a powerful but unloving, unjust, and capricious Master. This view was likely colored by Job's own actions as an unloving and unjust master, as evidenced by how those who served him had abandoned him. It appears that Job projected his own classist belief system onto God.

---

150. Job 7:1-3.

Chapter 5

GOD'S INJUSTICE

"Would you discredit my justice?
Would you condemn me to justify yourself?"

—GOD'S QUESTIONS TO JOB
Job 40:8

Horatio Gates Spafford was a prominent American lawyer, a senior partner in a large and thriving law firm, and a Presbyterian church elder active in the abolitionist movement. Spafford invested a great deal of his wealth in real estate and lost it in the Great Chicago Fire of 1871.[151] Scarlet fever took his young son of four from him. Two years later, in 1873, he sent his family ahead of him for a holiday to hear his friend, the great evangelist D. L. Moody, preach in England. While Spafford attended to business affairs that delayed his own arrival in England, an iron sailing vessel struck the ship carrying his wife and four daughters. His daughters—11-year-old Annie, 9-year-old Maggie, 5-year-old Bessie, and 2-year-old Tanetta—perished. His wife alone was spared.

Out of Spafford's great agony of spirit was penned one of the greatest hymns of all time:

---

151. Library of Congress, The American Colony in Jerusalem, Family Tragedy.
https://www.loc.gov/exhibits/americancolony/amcolony-family.html

When peace, like a river, attendeth my way,
When sorrows like sea billows roll;
Whatever my lot, Thou hast taught me to say,
It is well, it is well with my soul.

(Refrain:) It is well (it is well),
with my soul (with my soul),
It is well, it is well with my soul.

Though Satan should buffet,
though trials should come,
Let this blest assurance control,
That Christ hath regarded my helpless estate,
And hath shed His own blood for my soul.

My sin, oh the bliss of this glorious thought!
My sin, not in part but the whole,
Is nailed to His cross, and I bear it no more,
Praise the Lord, praise the Lord, O my soul!

For me, be it Christ, be it Christ hence to live:
If Jordan above me shall roll,
No pain shall be mine, for in death as in life
Thou wilt whisper Thy peace to my soul.

And Lord haste the day, when the faith shall be sight,
The clouds be rolled back as a scroll;
The trump shall resound, and the Lord shall descend,
Even so, it is well with my soul.

Absolute surrender. Contentment. Forgiveness. This peace amidst the storm comes only through the Spirit of God. None of us can achieve such a state on our own.

Compare Spafford's deep humility and understanding of his sinful estate amidst his suffering[152] with Job's claims of innocence.

Compare Spafford's refrain "it is well with my soul" with Job's complaint that all *was* well with him before God shattered him, seized him by the neck, and crushed him.[153]

Compare Spafford's recognition that God's supernatural peace melts earthly sorrow, so short-lived compared to the expanse of eternity, with Job's agonizingly pessimistic view toward his future on earth. Despite his initial noble words, Job lapsed into despair, as most of us would. He said:

I wish I were never born.[154]
I want to die.[155]
I prefer strangling and death, rather than this body of mine.[156]

---

152. Years later, Spafford and his wife, Anna, founded a controversial community in Israel. Whatever one's views of that controversy, his hymn suggests a faithful connection to God amidst his time of great sorrow.
153. Job 16:12: "All was well with me, but He shattered me; He seized me by the neck and crushed me."
154. Job 3:3-4: "May the day of my birth perish, and the night that said, 'A boy is conceived!' That day—may it turn to darkness; may God above not care about it; may no light shine on it."
155. Job 6:8-9: "Oh, that I might have my request, that God would grant what I hope for, that God would be willing to crush me, to let loose His hand and cut off my life!"
156. Job 7:15: "So that I prefer strangling and death, rather than this body of mine."

What profit did I gain by trying to please God?[157]
What do I gain by not sinning?[158]
My eyes will never see happiness again.[159]
Let me alone.[160]

Job has been rightly lauded throughout the centuries for persevering amidst his sorrow and clinging to his belief in a powerful God. He could have worshipped the sun and moon, as many did in his day, but he did not. Nor did he consort with mediums or call upon magic spells to help him. Most of all, Job did not abandon his faith or give up. In a choice that has comforted untold numbers of people in suffering, Job remembered his Redeemer and looked forward to an afterlife with God.

But Job was not blameless. He was arrogant. He was self-centered. And he was not patient, as he himself acknowledged, when he said, "What strength do I have, that I should still hope? What prospects, that I should be patient?"[161] Although in the beginning, Job did not charge God with wrongdoing,[162] he certainly did as time went on.[163] He lashed out at God for not listening to him and being distant.

Why do you hide Your face and consider me Your enemy?[164]

---

157. Job 34:9: "For he says, 'There is no profit in trying to please God.'"
158. Job 35:3: "Yet you ask Him, 'What profit is it to me, and what do I gain by not sinning?'"
159. Job 7:7: "My eyes will never see happiness again."
160. Job 7:16: "I despise my life; I would not live forever. Let me alone; my days have no meaning."
161. Job 6:11.
162. Job 1:22: "In all this, Job did not sin by charging God with wrongdoing."
163. Job 19:6: "Then know that God has wronged me and drawn His net around me."
164. Job 13:24.

I cry out to you, God, but You do not answer . . . .[165]
Even if I summoned Him and He responded, I do not
believe He would give me a hearing.[166]

Job accused God of acting capriciously, without rhyme or
reason.

He would crush me with a storm and multiply my
wounds for no reason.[167]

Job accused God of acting without pity or compassion on
him—in essence, not loving him.

You turn on me ruthlessly.[168]
He counts me among His enemies.[169]
Without pity, He pierces my kidneys and spills my
gall on the ground.[170]

Job viewed God as powerful, but angry.

God assails me and tears me in His anger and gnashes
His teeth at me.[171]
He moves mountains without their knowing it and
overturns them in His anger.[172]
God does not restrain His anger . . . .[173]
You bring new witnesses against me and increase

---

165. Job 30:20.
166. Job 9:16.
167. Job 9:17.
168. Job 30:21.
169. Job 19:11.
170. Job 16:13.
171. Job 16:9.
172. Job 9:5.
173. Job 9:13.

> *Your anger toward me; Your forces come against me*
> *wave upon wave.*[174]

Most of all, Job charged God with being unjust, rewarding the wicked and punishing the innocent.

> *As surely as God lives, who has denied me justice, the*
> *Almighty, who has made my life bitter.*[175]
> *He destroys both the blameless and the wicked.*[176]
> *He mocks the despair of the innocent.*[177]
> *Does it please you to oppress me, to spurn the work*
> *of Your hands, while You smile on the plans of the*
> *wicked?*[178]

Job held a worldview that the way to obtain God's blessing was through good works and that he gained his wealth, power, health, and acclaim **because** of his righteousness. This worldview is called "The Calculus" by the Rev. Dr. John Sittema, retired President and Chief Executive Officer of WorldServe Ministries and a pastor for 39 years.[179]

To understand the Calculus, one must understand the types of good works and when they come into play.

The first type consists of good works of "the flesh,"[180] when we

---

174. Job 10:17.
175. Job 27:2.
176. Job 9:22.
177. Job 9:23.
178. Job 10:3.
179. To hear the heart-rending story of how the Rev. John Sittema and his late wife, Sue, suffered from leukemia together, visit http://www.firstpersoninterview.com/john-sittema/.
180. According to the NIV note on Galatians 5:13, the Greek word for *flesh* (*sarx*) refers to the sinful state of human beings, often presented as a power in opposition to the Spirit.

operate under our own strength to win approval and blessings from God. These good works often have a ceremonial element to them. They may be performed publically, permitting us to win praise from others, and they often feed our religious pride. We may also perform them humbly in the sincere, but mistaken, belief that they will win us a place in eternity.

The second type of good works emanates from the Spirit. They are its fruit. Directed by the Lord and used for His purposes, they are marked by supernaturally bestowed patience, peace, and love,[181] even in great suffering or amidst extreme hatred. They are frequently accompanied by miracles orchestrated by the Invisible Hand. Importantly, they come *after* reunion with God, not before, and are proof of our relationship with Him.[182] Their hallmark is humility.

When Job demanded that the Lord go toe-to-toe with him about his level of righteousness, the Lord refused, because to do so would indicate that He accepted the Calculus, the Rev. Sittema says. Instead, He showed Job the real reason to worship Him and perform good works: "We worship God not so that He will bless us; we worship God because He is God, He is worthy, and His purposes are both just and loving," says the Rev. Sittema. "And that stops our mouths in awe."[183]

For the cosmic Calculus—the belief that good works earn our way to Heaven—is flawed.

---

181. Galatians 5:22-23: "But the fruit of the Spirit is love, joy, peace, forbearance, kindness, goodness, faithfulness, gentleness and self-control. Against such things there is no law."
182. James 2:17: "In the same way, faith by itself, if it is not accompanied by action, is dead."
183. This information was relayed directly to the author of this book.

Its first problem is that we can never know how many good works are enough and how many evil ones merit damnation. Therefore, like a hamster on a wheel, no matter how hard we work, we will never know whether we are reaching our destination. And this creates fear, anguish, and uncertainty. Whatever good works Job did, he did because he "dreaded destruction" from God.[184]

The second problem with the cosmic Calculus is that it does not address the condition of the heart. The Pharisees in the New Testament believed that they followed the Old Testament Law and regulations perfectly, but they had no friendship with God. They did not know Him,[185] nor did they have mercy for their fellow companions on life's journey. Consequently, they not only endangered themselves and others, but they lost out on the joy of being directed and empowered by the Spirit to perform acts that fit into a larger purpose.

The third, and most obvious problem with the cosmic Calculus is that mankind *cannot* be perfectly good. At different times, in different ways, and to different degrees, we are all narcissistic and proud. And that's just the beginning of our unrighteous deeds. For many of us, there is a great deal more. God, meanwhile, is righteous and holy—and holiness cannot tolerate even an atom of evil or it is no longer holy. Its pure essence becomes compromised and polluted.

---

184. Job 31:23: "For I dreaded destruction from God, and for fear of his splendor I could not do such things."

185. Matthew 7:22-23: "Many will say to me on that day, 'Lord, Lord, did we not prophesy in Your name and in Your name drive out demons and in Your name perform many miracles?' Then I will tell them plainly, 'I never knew you. Away from me, you evildoers!'"

How, then, can a Holy God and evil man be reconciled?

In Biblical times, the way to atone for one's evil acts was to repent and to offer sacrifices to the gods or to God, depending on in which entity one believed. Offering sacrifices for sin typically involved burning an animal. In pagan cults, the evil gods, which were demons,[186] demanded the burning of children to appease their anger, a practice the Lord forcefully renounced.[187]

But sacrifices demanded by the law did nothing to address the heart. Nor did they bring their offerors into friendship with God. It was an empty[188] way of life. Furthermore, sacrifices had to be given repeatedly. Alas, a more permanent solution was needed.

The book of Job masterfully establishes this dilemma and, in doing so, foreshadows the coming of Christ. Job calls for a Mediator,[189] a Redeemer-Defender[190] and an intercessor in Heaven who argues on his behalf.[191] Elihu joined Job when

---

186. I Corinthians 10:20: "No, but the sacrifices of pagans are offered to demons, not to God, and I do not want you to be participants with demons."

187. Jeremiah 32:35: "They built high places for Baal in the Valley of Ben Hinnom to sacrifice their sons and daughters to Molek, though I never commanded—nor did it enter my mind—that they should do such a detestable thing and so make Judah sin."

188. I Peter 1:18-19: "For you know that it was not with perishable things such as silver or gold that you were redeemed from the empty way of life handed down to you from your ancestors, but with the precious blood of Christ, a lamb without blemish or defect."

189. Job 9:33: "If only there were someone to mediate between us, someone to bring us together . . . ."

190. Job 19:25: "I know that my Redeemer lives, and that in the end He will stand on the earth."

191. Job 16:19-22: "Even now my witness is in heaven; my advocate is on high. My intercessor is my friend as my eyes pour out tears to God, on behalf of a man He pleads with God as one pleads for a friend."

he spoke of the discovery of a ransom that would spare people from going down to the pit.[192]

When Christ came to earth, He became both the sacrifice[193] and the prophesied ransom.[194] In doing so, He served a cosmic cause: By substituting Himself for sinful man, He met the demands of perfect holiness for justice. That mediation brought mankind back to its Creator.[195] By becoming the sacrifice, the Lord condescended Himself to operating in a language man understood. The price of admission to this new relationship was faith and submission to Jesus Christ.

In the process, Christ sought to reconcile two disparate groups: Jews and Gentiles, the ancient and alienated siblings of the Old Testament. The Apostle Paul put it this way: "For He Himself is our peace, who has made the two groups one and has destroyed the barrier, the dividing wall of hostility, by setting aside in His flesh the law with its commands and regulations. His purpose was to create in Himself one new humanity out of the two, thus making peace . . . . For through Him we both have access to the Father by one Spirit."[196]

---

192. Job 33:23-24: "Yet if there is an angel at their side, a messenger, one out of a thousand, sent to tell them how to be upright, and he is gracious to that person and says to God, 'Spare them from going down to the pit; I have found a ransom for them.'"

193. Romans 3:23-25: "For all have sinned and fall short of the glory of God, and all are justified freely by His grace through the redemption that came by Christ Jesus. God presented Christ as a sacrifice of atonement, through the shedding of his blood—to be received by faith."

194. Mark 10:45: "For even the Son of Man did not come to be served, but to serve, and to give His life as a ransom for many."

195. I Timothy 2:5: "For there is one God and one mediator between God and mankind, the man Christ Jesus."

196. Ephesians 2:14-18.

Although seemingly an odd way to reconcile man and God, the "blood" of Christ's death represents the humble dying to self, that is, self-sacrifice to give way to the purposes of God, according to the Christian author Andrew Murray. Life in the Spirit, which provides a taste of supernatural peace, follows. "The blood is the life of man; the Spirit is the life of God," Murray writes. "The outpouring of the blood rendered possible the outpouring of the Spirit."[197]

Job and his first three friends believed in the Calculus. Job argued he was good enough to merit reward; his friends argued he was not. When Job's underlying belief system was shaken, Job did what many of us would do in the face of such agony: Job turned his anger against God.

The Lord was not pleased with him. In a powerful one-line statement, He said to Job, "Would you condemn me to justify yourself?"[198]

The story of Job compels us to decide whom we believe: God or Job before he repented? For the logical conclusion of ascribing righteousness to Job is ascribing injustice to God. If we side with Job over God and insist that Job was righteous, we repeat his presumptuous error—the same error

---

197. "The blood is the life of man; the Spirit is the life of God. Man must sacrifice his sinful life, bear the penalty of his sin, and surrender himself entirely to God before God could dwell in him with His life. What man himself could not do, that the Lord Jesus, the Son of Man did for him. He shed His blood, He gave His life in entire surrender to the will of God as a satisfaction of the penalty of sin. When that was accomplished, it was possible for Him to receive the Spirit from the Father that He might pour Him out. The outpouring of the blood rendered possible the outpouring of the Spirit." Murray, Andrew. *The Blood of the Cross*. (New Kensington, Pennsylvania, USA, Whitaker House, 1981), 13.

198. Job 40:8.

that invited the Lord's memorable and devastating rebuke. If we champion Job's blamelessness, we reject the Scriptures that state those who claim to be blameless are deceived. If we accept Job's version of events, we also accept his worldview of the Calculus.

The traditional interpretation of the book of Job presents yet another danger. It suggests that God's ways are shrouded in mystery—that we suffer through random events and will never know why. Acquiescing to this premise too quickly stops us from seeking His face, a vital process in spiritual growth that can take decades. The Lord *wants* to explain to us life's ambiguities,[199] but attributing all to mystery prevents us from persisting in this transformative quest for understanding.[200] In contrast, if we ask and expect Him to answer, the Spirit of wisdom and revelation will show us more than we can imagine,[201] even if it takes nearly a lifetime, as it did with Moses and Joseph.

In his sermon, "Why God Waits to Answer our Prayers," the late Rev. David Wilkerson gives a profound answer to the important question of why God waits to answer prayers:

---

199. Matthew 7:7-8: "Ask and it will be given to you; seek and you will find; knock and the door will be opened to you. For everyone who asks receives; the one who seeks finds; and to the one who knocks, the door will be opened."

200. James 1:5-8: "If any of you lacks wisdom, you should ask God, who gives generously to all without finding fault, and it will be given to you. But when you ask, you must believe and not doubt, because the one who doubts is like a wave of the sea, blown and tossed by the wind. That person should not expect to receive anything from the Lord. Such a person is double-minded and unstable in all they do."

201. Ephesians 1:17: "I keep asking that the God of our Lord Jesus Christ, the glorious Father, may give you the Spirit of wisdom and revelation, so that you may know Him better."

Because in the process of suffering, it takes time for us to surrender absolutely to Him.[202] In other words, we are the ones moving slowly, not He.

In his own excruciating period of waiting, Job eventually came to understand that the Lord, in permitting him to suffer, was molding him for his own salvation.

It was the lesson that Job needed to hear.

---

202. Wilkerson, David. "Why God Waits to Answer Our Prayers," Times Square Church Pulpit Series, Manhattan, New York, New York. See https://www.youtube.com/watch?v=9O18t4Tux30

Chapter 6

ELEPHANT IN
THE ROOM

"He was a murderer from the beginning,
not holding to the truth, for there is no truth in him.
When he lies, he speaks his native language,
for he is a liar and the father of lies."

—*JESUS CHRIST*
John 8:44

In all his complaints that God was unfair—understandable from a human point of view, but unthinkable[203] from a Spirit-filled point of view—never once does Job recognize or rail against the real enemy. Satan, in typical fashion, remains anonymous in Job's world, delighted to let God take the fall for his evil handiwork. Satan, commander of legions of demons, is the proverbial elephant in the room.

In fact, Job thought about injustice in the world—and then, amazingly, blamed God for it. "When a land falls into the hands of the wicked, [God] blindfolds its judges. If it is not He, then who is it?" Job said.[204] The correct answer, of course, is Satan, the deceiver, tempter, murderer, and adversary of God from the beginning.

---

203. Job 34:12: "It is unthinkable that God would do wrong, that the Almighty would pervert justice."
204. Job 9:24.

Who is Satan?

The book of Ezekiel tells us that Satan was a guardian cherub, "the seal of perfection, full of wisdom and perfect in beauty" in Eden, the garden of God. He was adorned with every precious stone: carnelian, chrysolite, emerald, topaz, onyx, jasper, lapis lazuli, turquoise, and beryl. The settings and mountings of his jewels were made of gold. God showered and anointed this grand spirit with all the splendor of heaven. From the day he was created, he was blameless. Then the guardian cherub, called "Lucifer,"[205] became proud because of his beauty. Given free will by God, he misused his power and denounced the source of his extraordinary gifts. As a result, Satan was thrown to earth.[206] Angels who followed him were not spared.[207]

---

205. Isaiah 14:12 (KJV): "How art thou fallen from heaven, O Lucifer, son of the morning! How art thou cut down to the ground, which didst weaken the nations!"

206. Ezekiel 28:12-17: "'You were the seal of perfection, full of wisdom and perfect in beauty. You were in Eden, the garden of God; every precious stone adorned you: carnelian, chrysolite and emerald, topaz, onyx and jasper, lapis lazuli, turquoise and beryl. Your settings and mountings were made of gold; on the day you were created they were prepared. You were anointed as a guardian cherub, for so I ordained you. You were on the holy mount of God; you walked among the fiery stones. You were blameless in your ways from the day you were created till wickedness was found in you. Through your widespread trade you were filled with violence, and you sinned. So I drove you in disgrace from the mount of God, and I expelled you, guardian cherub, from among the fiery stones. Your heart became proud on account of your beauty, and you corrupted your wisdom because of your splendor. So I threw you to the earth; I made a spectacle of you before kings."

207. 2 Peter 2:4: "For if God did not spare angels when they sinned, but sent them to hell, putting them in chains of darkness to be held for judgment . . ." Jude 1:6: "And the angels who did not keep their positions of authority but abandoned their proper dwelling—these he has kept in darkness, bound with everlasting chains for judgment on the great Day."

This great conflict in heaven was a familiar story to Eliphaz. Twice, Eliphaz referenced the Lord charging his angels with error.[208] These could not have been "good angels," because nowhere else does Scripture suggest that they erred. The reference must have been to fallen angels, those for whom eternal fire is prepared.[209] Although Eliphaz recognized these demonic forces, Job, in all his many words,[210] did not.

In his book, *The Christian in Complete Armour,* William Gurnall states that the invisibility of the devil and his demons makes them little feared by the ignorant world. The result for Job was that he "had fallen into the snare of the devil," according to the Rev. John Fry,[211] an English Rector who authored the 1827 book, *A New Translation and Exposition of the Very Ancient Book of Job.*

Job saw the world through the fictitious lens that Satan masterfully created for him. Job was righteous and others

---

208. Job 4:18-19: "If God places no trust in His servants, if He charges his angels with error, how much more those who live in houses of clay, whose foundations are in the dust, who are crushed more readily than a moth!" Job 15:15-16: "If God places no trust in His holy ones, if even the heavens are not pure in His eyes, how much less mortals, who are vile and corrupt, who drink up evil like water!"

209. Matthew 25:41: "Then He will say to those on his left, 'Depart from me, you who are cursed, into the eternal fire prepared for the devil and his angels.'"

210. Job 8:2: "How long will you say such things? Your words are a blustering wind." Job 11:2: "Are all these words to go unanswered? Is this talker to be vindicated?" Job 35:16: "So Job opens his mouth with empty talk; without knowledge he multiplies words."

211. The Rev. John Fry, B.A. *A New Translation and Exposition of the Very Ancient Book of Job: with Notes,* (London, England, Nabu Press, Printed for James Duncan, 37, Paternoster-Row, 1827), 457. The Rev. Fry was of University College, Oxford, and a Rector in Desford, Leicestershire, England. He authored at least seven books.

were not. Job deserved blessings such as wealth and health, and others did not. Job merited universal adulation while his enemies were less than human, not worthy to place with his sheep dogs. Job's friends let him down. Job's relatives let him down. Job's servants let him down. Most of all, God let him down.

Like all of us in different times or in different aspects of our lives, Job was gripped by a powerful delusion. And he was blinded to Satan's schemes.

In contrast to Job, Horatio Gates Spafford knew the source of his troubles. He named the enemy. *"Though Satan should buffet . . ."* reads a verse in his beloved hymn, "When Peace Like a River." He wrote the hymn on a ship while passing over the place where his daughters had drowned.[212]

After losing her family in Nazi Germany and being imprisoned herself in German death camps, Corrie ten Boom penned a book on spiritual warfare called *Defeated Enemies*. She wrote the book in the belief that many believers are surrounded by the powers of darkness, the devil, and demons, but do not recognize them or understand how to deal with them.[213]

The Old Testament prophet Daniel was informed that a supernatural clash with "The Prince[214] of Persia"—a reference

---

212. Library of Congress, The American Colony in Jerusalem, Family Tragedy. https://www.loc.gov/exhibits/americancolony/amcolony-family.html
213. Ten Boom, Corrie. *Defeated Enemies*, (Fort Washington, PA, CLC Publications, 2012), 1.
214. The word "Prince" in this verse can also mean "patron-angel" or "ruler of rulers (of God)," according to the *King James Version*, Old Testament Hebrew Lexicon, part of the Interlinear Bible.

to a demonic force, according to Biblical scholars, and a representation of the "principalities"[215] against which we struggle—delayed the angelic help assigned to him.[216] The Apostle Paul, too, spoke of a delay caused by Satan[217] and taught his followers to be aware of Satan's schemes.[218]

The Apostle Peter warned his community not to fall into the hands of the predator, who prowls like a roaring lion looking for someone to devour.[219] Peter undoubtedly gained insight from the times he himself fell prey to Satan. For even after recognizing Christ as the Son of God, Peter cooperated with Satan's view of the world and insisted that Jesus shun the suffering to which He was destined. Jesus rebuked him. "Get behind me, Satan!" He said. "You do not have in mind the concerns of God, but merely human concerns."[220] Satan, often called the "Great Humanist," had convinced Peter to place human comfort (and possibly political goals) ahead of

See http://www.biblestudytools.com/lexicons/hebrew/kjv/sar.html

215. Ephesians 6:12: (KJV) "For we wrestle not against flesh and blood, but against principalities, against powers, against the rulers of the darkness of this world, against spiritual wickedness in high places."

216. Daniel 10:12-13: "Then he continued, 'Do not be afraid, Daniel. Since the first day that you set your mind to gain understanding and to humble yourself before your God, your words were heard, and I have come in response to them. But the prince of the Persian kingdom resisted me twenty-one days. Then Michael, one of the chief princes, came to help me, because I was detained there with the king of Persia.'"

217. 1 Thessalonians 2:18: "For we wanted to come to you—certainly I, Paul, did, again and again—but Satan blocked our way."

218. 2 Corinthians 2:11: ". . . in order that Satan might not outwit us. For we are not unaware of his schemes."

219. 1 Peter 5:8: "Be alert and of sober mind. Your enemy the devil prowls around like a roaring lion looking for someone to devour."

220. Matthew 16:22-23: "Peter took him aside and began to rebuke him. 'Never, Lord!' he said. 'This shall never happen to you!' Jesus turned and said to Peter, 'Get behind me, Satan! You are a stumbling block to me; you do not have in mind the concerns of God, but merely human concerns.'"

the purposes of God. While the Great Commandment states, "Love the Lord your God with all your heart and with all your soul and with all your mind," humanism elevates the second commandment, which states, "Love your neighbor as yourself,"[221] to first place. In humanism, man's view of the world, human comfort, and human feelings are more important than God's purposes.

Some theologians believe that the entity who challenged the Lord to test Job's righteousness was not Satan, but an angel of light. They argue that the heavenly being could not have been Satan because Satan would not have reported to God. In his 1827 book on Job, however, the Rev. Fry sees no contradiction in recognizing the entity as Satan and "the absolute dependence of angelic beings, be they good or evil, on the will of God in all their actings towards men . . . ."[222] Furthermore, Job 2:1 does not say that Satan came as one of the angels, but rather that he came *with them*.

The Rev. Fry states that although we may not fully understand the origin of evil, "the Scripture does plainly trace it all to one father and one author, who stood forth as the adversary of his Creator, the head of the angelic hosts; and did prevail, we know, to withdraw angels and principalities and powers from the truth of their allegiance, and to corrupt mankind in their first parents as soon as created."[223]

Furthermore, the Satan of Job 1:6 visited sickness and destruction onto Job—a trademark of the devil, not God,

---

221. Matthew 22:37-39.
222. Fry, *A New Translation*. Preface, xix.
223. Ibid, 63.

who designed the earth to be good[224] before the Serpent's temptations created the great fall. In the work of Christ and his Apostles, sickness was frequently associated with Satan, his demons, and sin.[225]

Others argue that the entity in Job 1 was indeed Satan, but he was still in Heaven and had not yet evolved into the evil and powerful being of the New Testament. These commentators argue that the Satan of the book of Job was not yet a fallen angel. However, such an argument contradicts the report that Satan was expelled from Eden, the garden of God,[226] after "wickedness was found in [him]."[227] Furthermore, in Job 1:7, Satan states that he returned "from roaming throughout the earth, going back and forth on it." By then, the earth was already Satan's assigned territory.[228] Although the character of Satan may have been revealed in greater detail in the New Testament, Scripture makes clear that Satan's character did not change. In John 8:44, Jesus Christ refers to the devil as being a murderer "from the beginning, not holding to the truth, for there is no truth in him," suggesting consistency

---

224. Genesis 1.
225. Luke 13:16: "Then should not this woman, a daughter of Abraham, whom Satan has kept bound for eighteen long years, be set free on the Sabbath day from what bound her?" Mark 5:15: "When they came to Jesus, they saw the man who had been possessed by the legion of demons, sitting there, dressed and in his right mind; and they were afraid." Luke 9:1: "When Jesus had called the Twelve together, he gave them power and authority to drive out all demons and to cure diseases." 2 Corinthians 12:7 "Therefore, in order to keep me from becoming conceited, I was given a thorn in my flesh, a messenger of Satan, to torment me."
226. Ezekiel 28:13: "You were in Eden, the garden of God . . . ."
227. Ezekiel 28:15: "You were blameless in your ways from the day you were created till wickedness was found in you."
228. Ezekiel 28:17: "So I threw you to the earth; I made a spectacle of you before kings."

in character between the Old Testament (called the "First Testament" by some scholars) and the New Testament. In Genesis 3, the serpent was an adversary of God when he challenged the truthfulness of God and successfully tempted God's created people to disobey him. Revelation 12:9 refers to the devil, or Satan, who leads the whole world astray,[229] as the "ancient serpent."

Yet others argue that the conversation between God and Satan indicates that the entire book of Job is a parable, a historical novel, or an allegory. However, the book contains very specific geographical references and family lines, atypical for parables or allegories. While novels are action-filled, this book contains mostly conversations. Furthermore, other authors—such as the prophet Ezekiel, the New Testament Apostle James, and the Jewish writer Josephus—refer to Job as a real person, Fry states in his argument for historical authenticity.[230] Final evidence is that Satan talks with God elsewhere in the Bible.[231] In one such event, Satan approaches the Lord to request permission to sift the Apostles like wheat.[232] Although we are not privy to that conversation, the similarities to Job are remarkable. In both cases, Satan requests permission to afflict God's followers. Therefore, if Satan's request to God makes the

---

229. Rev. 12:9: "The great dragon was hurled down—that ancient serpent called the devil, or Satan, who leads the whole world astray. He was hurled to the earth, and his angels with him."
230. Fry, *A New Translation*. Preface, v.
231. Zechariah 3:1-2: "Then he showed me Joshua the high priest standing before the angel of the Lord, and Satan standing at his right side to accuse him. The Lord said to Satan, "The Lord rebuke you, Satan! . . . " Mark 1:13: "[Jesus] was in the wilderness forty days, being tempted by Satan."
232. Luke 22:31: "Simon, Simon, Satan has asked to sift all of you as wheat."

book of Job a historical novel, then logic requires that the book of Luke be considered one as well.

No, in fact, Satan is a real and consistent presence in the Old and the New Testaments. The one who attempts to remove him from Scripture or trivialize his presence does so at his own peril.

The story of Job provides deep insight into how Satan leads mankind astray. For Job, it began with his utter failure to recognize the true enemy, with whom he unwittingly cooperated. There were other means of diverting him from his path.

First, Job opened himself up to exaggeration, little "white lies" that placed him squarely in the territory of the devil. Job exaggerated his benevolence when he stated that he guided widows from his birth and fathered the fatherless from his youth. Although he claimed to have been the benefactor of all those who hungered, the presence of the starving and mocking young men who lived in the riverbeds suggests otherwise. His representations that he treated his family, friends, and servants well does not comport with the accounts of his friends, or with their universal absence in his time of need.

Second, Job sought the praise of men. His entire identity was built on being respected. When that rock was moved, he was devastated. Job longed for the days when he took his seat in the public square, when the young men stepped aside, when old men rose to their feet, and when everyone revered him (or so he thought) in silent awe, listening for his wise counsel.

Third, Job's business practices, fueled by greed, were of great concern to the Lord. By taking houses he did not build, he appropriated wealth that he did not earn. As a lender, Job required pledges from borrowers—his relatives—for no reason. Although a powerful and honored landowner, Job stripped people of their clothing, left them naked, and abused his power by withholding food and water from those who needed it. He sent widows away empty-handed and broke the strength of the fatherless. Unethical business practices perpetrated by religious people are one of Satan's most effective means for turning humanity away from God and from His church. In a curious description of the epic fall of Satan from heaven, the Scriptures state that the winged cherub, once glorious, engaged in oppressive business practices.[233] Those who fall into Satan's snare adopt his ways.

In contrast, "Quaker Capitalism" of the Nineteenth Century—the likes of which built the early chocolate empires—was founded on the idea that wealth creation was not only for the entrepreneurs, but for the benefit of the workers, the local community, and society as large, writes Deborah Cadbury, a descendent of the Quakers of Cadbury chocolate, in her book, *The Chocolate Wars: The 150-Year Rivalry between the World's Greatest Chocolate Makers*. The idea that wealth creation was only for personal gain would have been offensive to the Quakers, who built businesses based on a strict code of ethics while writing groundbreaking papers on pov-

---

233. Ezekiel 28:16 (CEB): "But because of your trade, your oppressive business practices piled up, and you became impure. So I expelled you from God's mountain. I removed you, winged creature, guardian, from among the stones of fire."

erty, publishing authoritative studies of the Bible, and cam-
paigning against the heart-rending human rights abuses in a
world that seemed straight out of Dickens, Cadbury writes.[234]

Fourth, Job turned off the soundings of his own
conscience when he said, "my conscience will not reproach
me as long as I live."[235] Listening to the whispers of the soul is
critical to enjoy communion with God.

Fifth, even before his devastation, Job was driven by fear,
the opposite of faith. Since he was unaware of Satan's schemes,
Job did not know how to protect himself against them.
"Resist the devil and he will flee from you," James 4:7 states.
While faith is the proper shield to protect against Satan's
arrows,[236] Job conceded that prior to the catastrophic events
that befell him, he dreaded destruction, a common state of
mind for those living outside of God's values and for those
who do not believe God loves them. "What I feared has come
upon me; what I dreaded has happened to me," he said.[237]
In Job 31:23, he reiterated that dread.[238] After the disasters,
Job's fears turned to terror.[239] Because we are inherently
unreliable and events are outside our control, we will never

---

234. Cadbury, Deborah. *The Chocolate Wars: The 150-Year Rivalry between
the World's Greatest Chocolate Makers.* (New York: PublicAffairs™, a
member of the Perseus Books Group, 2010), Introduction, xi.
235. Job 27:6.
236. Ephesians 6:16: "In addition to all this, take up the shield of faith, with
which you can extinguish all the flaming arrows of the evil one."
237. Job 3:25.
238. Job 31:23: "For I dreaded destruction from God, and for fear of His
splendor I could not do such things."
239. Job 6:4: "The arrows of the Almighty are in me, my spirit drinks in their
poison; God's terrors are marshaled against me." Job 7:13-14: "When I
think my bed will comfort me and my couch will ease my complaint, even
then you frighten me with dreams and terrify me with visions . . . ."

feel secure when we rely on ourselves or our possessions.[240] Insecurity and fear drive ego and, thus, many of the world's greatest blunders.

Sixth, Job opened himself up to envy. In Psalm 73:4-11, the Psalmist describes how he, the Psalmist, nearly lost his foothold, and how his feet had nearly slipped because he envied the arrogant when he saw their prosperity.

> *They have no struggles; their bodies are healthy and strong. They are free from common human burdens; they are not plagued by human ills. Therefore, pride is their necklace; they clothe themselves with violence. From their callous hearts comes iniquity; their evil imaginations have no limits. They scoff, and speak with malice; with arrogance they threaten oppression. Their mouths lay claim to heaven, and their tongues take possession of the earth. Therefore, their people turn to them and drink up waters in abundance. They say, "How would God know? Does the Most High know anything?"*

Compare the Psalmist's words with Job's:

> *Why do the wicked live on, growing old and increasing in power? They see their children established around them, their offspring before their eyes. Their homes are safe and free from fear; the rod of God is not on them. Their bulls never fail to*

---

240. Psalm 33:16-18: "No king is saved by the size of his army; no warrior escapes by his great strength. A horse is a vain hope for deliverance; despite all its great strength it cannot save. But the eyes of the Lord are on those who fear Him, on those whose hope is in His unfailing love."

breed; their cows calve and do not miscarry. They send forth their children as a flock; their little ones dance about. They sing to the music of timbrel and lyre; they make merry to the sound of the pipe. They spend their years in prosperity and go down to the grave in peace. Yet they say to God, "Leave us alone! We have no desire to know Your ways."[241]

Although there is remarkable similarity between the sentiments of the Psalmist and of Job, there is one great difference: Job did not catch himself and denounce his wrong-headed thinking. The Psalmist did.

In a chapter referencing leadership in the church, the Apostle James calls bitter envy a sin that, coupled with selfish ambition, leads to disorder and every evil practice.[242] Envy lies below the surface of an earthly wisdom that James calls demonic.[243] Such teachers have a form of godliness, but deny its power.[244] Envy drives achievement.[245] One sign of this phenomena is the counting of one's power base. At the urging of Satan, King David counted his men, resulting in

---

241. Job 21:7-14.

242. James 3:16: "For where you have envy and selfish ambition, there you find disorder and every evil practice."

243. James 3:13-15: "Who is wise and understanding among you? Let them show it by their good life, by deeds done in the humility that comes from wisdom. But if you harbor bitter envy and selfish ambition in your hearts, do not boast about it or deny the truth. Such 'wisdom' does not come down from heaven but is earthly, unspiritual, demonic."

244. 2 Timothy 3:5: "(H)aving a form of godliness but denying its power. Have nothing to do with such people." Verse 8 suggests these people were teachers.

245. Ecclesiastes 4:4. "And I saw that all toil and all achievement spring from one person's envy of another."

catastrophic consequences.[246] Contrast David's actions to Gideon, who obediently reduced the number of his followers from 32,000 to 300 to demonstrate that victory comes from the Lord. Twenty-two thousand of the followers that Gideon released were driven by fear.[247]

Like David, Job counted his power base: 7,000 sheep, 3,000 camels, 500 yoke of oxen, and 500 donkeys.[248] If it were not Job who ordered such a tally, who was it? Job's power, then, came not from servanthood and dependence on the Holy Spirit, but on the wealth his hands had gained.[249] Houses built like this are built in vain.[250] Like his other shortcomings, however, Job did not see it this way.

---

246. 2 Samuel 24:1 and 9-10 (KJ21): "And again the anger of the Lord was kindled against Israel, and he [Satan] moved David against them to say, "Go, number Israel and Judah . . . . And Joab gave the sum of the number of the people unto the king: and there were in Israel eight hundred thousand valiant men who drew the sword, and the men of Judah were five hundred thousand men. And David's heart smote him after he had numbered the people. And David said unto the Lord, 'I have sinned greatly in what I have done. And now, I beseech Thee, O Lord, take away the iniquity of Thy servant, for I have done very foolishly.'"

247. Judges 7:2-4 and 8: "The Lord said to Gideon, 'You have too many men. I cannot deliver Midian into their hands, or Israel would boast against me, 'My own strength has saved me.' Now announce to the army, 'Anyone who trembles with fear may turn back and leave Mount Gilead.' So twenty-two thousand men left, while ten thousand remained . . . . But the Lord said to Gideon, 'There are still too many men . . . .' So Gideon sent the rest of the Israelites home but kept the three hundred . . . ."

248. Job 1:3: "(A)nd he owned seven thousand sheep, three thousand camels, five hundred yoke of oxen and five hundred donkeys, and had a large number of servants. He was the greatest man among all the people of the East."

249. Job 31:25: "(I)f I have rejoiced over my great wealth, the fortune my hands had gained . . ."

250. Psalm 127:1: "Unless the Lord builds the house, the builders labor in vain."

Seventh, Job relied on religious ritual and works, not on friendship with God or the fruits of the Spirit, as his form of righteousness. His deeds were not loving and, thus, contradicted his words. In Matthew 7:22-23, Jesus speaks of the many on earth who carry the name of God, but do not know Him and will fail in the Judgment as a result. In the end, Job faced the sobering and humbling realization that he had only *heard* of God.

Eighth, after he emerged from his initial mourning period, it took a long time for Job to become silent before God, a process indispensable to seeking His face. Through the prophet Isaiah, the Lord told His people, "In repentance and rest is your salvation, in quietness and trust is your strength," but Job, like the people in the prophet's day, "would have none of it."[251] Job spoke with many words, like a "hot east wind,"[252] until he eventually confessed that he did not know what he was talking about.[253] Elihu stated that it is the breath of the Almighty that gives a person understanding.[254] The Spirit of God cannot speak when a man talks endlessly, clouding his ability to listen in silent expectation of revelation. It was only when Job became quiet that the Lord began to answer his questions.

---

251. Isaiah 30:15: "This is what the Sovereign Lord, the Holy One of Israel, says: 'In repentance and rest is your salvation, in quietness and trust is your strength, but you would have none of it.'"
252. Job 15:2-3 "Would a wise person answer with empty notions or fill their belly with the hot east wind? Would they argue with useless words, with speeches that have no value?"
253. Job 42:3 (NLT): "You asked, 'Who is this that questions my wisdom with such ignorance?' It is I—and I was talking about things I knew nothing about, things far too wonderful for me."
254. Job 32:8: "But it is the spirit in a person, the breath of the Almighty, that gives them understanding."

Ninth, Job claimed, except for committing sins in his youth,[255] to be blameless. 1 John 1:8 states, "If we claim to be without sin, we deceive ourselves and the truth is not in us." Job could not have been blameless, as he claimed, not only because it was impossible, but also because he had not been in true friendship with God, the ultimate and joyful outcome of his path of suffering.

Tenth, Job projected his own sin on others. Rather than examining himself, Job lashed out at his friends. Job blamed God for alienating him from his relatives when he himself was to blame. Proverbs 19:3 states, "A person's own folly leads to their ruin, yet their heart rages against the Lord." When blamed, the Lord was not amused and said to Job, "Would you discredit my justice? Would you condemn me to justify yourself?"[256] Man cannot have both free will and the right to blame God for the consequences of his own poor choices or the choices of others, either individually, as a community, as a nation, or as a planet. There are laws of cause and effect, and when we or our neighbors act wrongly, we experience negative effects. Like generations of parents who release their children into adulthood and sorrow when they choose treacherous paths, the Lord gives us freedom to fail and to suffer the consequences.[257]

Eleventh, while Job believed God was all powerful, he lost

---

255. Job 13:26: "For you write down bitter things against me and make me reap the sins of my youth."
256. Job 40:8.
257. Jeremiah 34:17: "Therefore this is what the Lord says: You have not obeyed me; you have not proclaimed freedom to your own people. So I now proclaim 'freedom' for you, declares the Lord—'freedom' to fall by the sword, plague and famine."

faith that God loved him. Elihu challenged this point when he said, "God is mighty but despises no one."[258] How we view God is the most critical question we will ever face. "And without faith it is impossible to please God, because anyone who comes to Him must believe that He exists and that He rewards those who earnestly seek him."[259] Job misunderstood the character of God. By characterizing God as capricious and unjust, he believed that God was untrustworthy and unloving. In reality, the Lord would never cause misery for His own amusement. God's thoughts, intentions, desires, and plans are always for our good and never for our harm, even when He permits us to suffer.[260]

Finally, and perhaps most importantly of all, Job fell into pride, a common failing in those with great skills, power, and wealth.[261] Like Satan, who lost his stature as the guardian cherub in heaven because he appropriated the gift of extreme beauty as his own, Job mistook God's gifts as if he were their source and they were designed to serve him alone. Job's belief system was based on the premise that because he was blessed, he must have been righteous, and this sign of favor with God gave him free rein to abuse those who had not been also blessed by God.

---

258. Job 36:5.
259. Hebrews 11:6.
260. Jeremiah 29:11: "'For I know the plans I have for you' declares the Lord, 'plans to prosper you and not to harm you, plans to give you hope and a future.'" James 1:17: "Every good and perfect gift is from above, coming down from the Father of the heavenly lights, who does not change like shifting shadows."
261. Ezekiel 28:4-5: "By your wisdom and understanding you have gained wealth for yourself and amassed gold and silver in your treasuries. By your great skill in trading you have increased your wealth, and because of your wealth your heart has grown proud."

Those who fall into Satan's deception take on not only his practices, but his characteristics. They see themselves as equal with God. When Job rebuked his friends for siding with God over him, he became victim to this deceit. "Will you speak wickedly on God's behalf? Will you speak deceitfully for Him? Will you show Him partiality? Will you argue the case for God?" Job said.[262]

Astonished at his audacity, Eliphaz responded, "You even undermine piety and hinder devotion to God . . . . Your own mouth condemns you, not mine; your own lips testify against you."[263]

Job's pride was of the worst kind—religious pride— which alienates untold numbers of people from the path toward God. In Matthew 23:13, Christ said that hypocritical teachers of the law "shut the door of the kingdom of heaven in people's faces" and they themselves do not enter.[264] The great Christian thinker C.S. Lewis said that the devil laughs when he can move a person from other vices to pride, the utmost evil, the vice that made the devil who he is. "He is perfectly content to see you becoming chaste and brave and self-controlled provided, all the time, he is setting up in you the Dictatorship of Pride," Lewis wrote. "For Pride is spiritual cancer; it eats up the very possibility of love, or contentment, or even common sense."[265]

---

262. Job 13:7-8.

263. Job 15:4-6.

264. Matthew 23:13: "Woe to you, teachers of the law and Pharisees, you hypocrites! You shut the door of the kingdom of heaven in people's faces. You yourselves do not enter, nor will you let those enter who are trying to."

265. C.S. Lewis, *Mere Christianity*, (San Francisco, HarperSanFrancisco, a Division of HarperCollins Publishers, 1952), 124-125.

The Rev. Fry put it this way: "Being lifted up with pride, [Job] had fallen into the snare of the devil, who had 'desired to have him, that he might sift him as wheat.' God had ordered that it should be so, not to gratify the malice of the devil, but to expose and correct in a child whom He loved something that did offend His heavenly eyes; and, no doubt, for an example to others, that those who think, that . . . they 'do righteousness' and 'love mercy,' may learn also 'to walk humbly with their God.'"[266]

---

266. Fry, *A New Translation*, 457.

Chapter 7

BREAKTHROUGH

"But whenever anyone turns to the Lord,
the veil is taken away."

—2 CORINTHIANS 3:16

D o you know people who talk about God continuously but, if stripped of the words and the ceremonies, would show no evidence of righteousness? They take advantage of their families and friends. They don't pay their bills or their workers. They steal through abusive business practices. They mock, they lie, and they cheat. All the while, they lead endless church activities and proudly wear the label of follower of God. Appearing clean on the outside, these modern-day false believers are full of greed, hypocrisy, jealousy, and self-indulgence inside—and blind to their own sins. While they represent themselves as children of God, they are, in reality, children of Satan.[267] They are masqueraders who bring the name of God into disrepute. In the Bible, Jesus described the religious leaders as these types of people.[268]

---

267. John 8:41-44: "'We are not illegitimate children,' they protested. 'The only Father we have is God himself.' Jesus said to them, 'If God were your Father, you would love Me, for I have come here from God. I have not come on my own; God sent Me. Why is my language not clear to you? Because you are unable to hear what I say. You belong to your father, the devil, and you want to carry out your father's desires . . . .'"
268. Matthew 23:25: "Woe to you, teachers of the law and Pharisees, you hypocrites! You clean the outside of the cup and dish, but inside they are full of greed and self-indulgence."

If we are honest with ourselves, we would all cringe in recognition of our flashes of unwarranted self-importance, countless number of sins, and blind spots. We all are arrogant, accusatory, judgmental, and narcissistic.

We are all like Job.

The question is whether we are willing to confess our sins and permit the Spirit to change us. Will we dull our consciences or draw closer to the light? In the light, the impurities in our souls become more visible, writes Andrew Murray in his book, *How to Strengthen Your Faith*.[269] Moses, a confidant of the Creator of the Universe, was humbler than anyone else on the face of the earth.[270]

In contrast, the further away we are from God, the greater the grand disconnect between how we view ourselves and reality.

This disconnect takes on many faces.

American college freshmen see themselves as more gifted than at any other time in history. Yet, by every objective indicator of student achievement, they fall far behind their international peers.[271] In the circles of power, countless

---

269. Andrew Murray, *How to Strengthen Your Faith*. (New Kensington, PA, Whitaker Press, 1977), 46-47.
270. Numbers 12:3: "(Now Moses was a very humble man, more humble than anyone else on the face of the earth.)"
271. For more than 50 years, the annual Freshman Survey administered by the Cooperative Institutional Research Program of the University of California, Los Angeles has provided data on incoming college students' background characteristics, high school experiences, attitudes, behaviors, and expectations for college. The survey, created by Dr. Alexander "Sandy" Astin in 1966, has resided at the Higher Education Research Institute at UCLA since 1973. To date, more than 15 million students at more than 1,900 institutions have participated in the survey.

politicians, members of the media, and entertainers have stumbled into self-deception that led to their destruction. In the field of psychology, the *Dunning–Kruger Effect* refers to illusory superiority, a condition wherein persons of low ability mistakenly assess their cognitive ability as greater than it is. Lacking self-awareness, they cannot objectively evaluate their actual competence or incompetence.

The Bible describes this phenomenon in a different way: Such deception comes from pride of one's heart. Obadiah 1:3 states, "The pride of your heart has deceived you . . . you who say to yourself, 'Who can bring me down to the ground?'"[272]

Breaking through such a blockage is a monumental challenge. In Job's case, losing his children did not bring him self-awareness. The destruction of his servants and animals did not open his eyes. The loss of his treasured stature in the community did not remove the impasse on the road to reality. Being imprisoned in a body wracked with pain did not release him from his "captivity."[273]

Job's three friends fervently and heroically—with no prospect of gain for themselves —tried to break through Job's self-deception in hopes that he would repent and be restored.[274]

---

272. See also Jeremiah 49:16: "The terror you inspire and the pride of your heart have deceived you . . . ." Ezekiel 28:2: "Son of man, say to the ruler of Tyre, 'This is what the Sovereign Lord says: 'In the pride of your heart you say, 'I am a god; I sit on the throne of a god in the heart of the seas.' But you are a mere mortal and not a god, though you think you are as wise as a god.'"

273. Job 42:10 (KJV): "And the Lord turned the captivity of Job, when he prayed for his friends . . . ."

274. Job 5:17-26: "Blessed is the one whom God corrects; so do not despise the discipline of the Almighty. For He wounds, but He also binds up; He injures, but His hands also heal. From six calamities He will rescue you; in seven no harm will touch you. In famine He will deliver you from death,

That did not work either. "So these three men stopped answering Job, because he was righteous in his own eyes."[275]

Only the young Elihu, who spoke in the Spirit,[276] began to make inroads, the indication of which was that although Elihu invited Job to defend himself, Job—for once—did not reply.[277]

What broke through?

Job, after becoming silent, met God, who had always been there, waiting for his child. In what the Rev. Fry calls an act of "great condescension,"[278] the Lord reasoned with His presumptuous creature. Job needed to understand that he was not equal with God. The Lord said:

---

and in battle from the stroke of the sword. You will be protected from the lash of the tongue, and need not fear when destruction comes. You will laugh at destruction and famine, and need not fear the wild animals. For you will have a covenant with the stones of the field, and the wild animals will be at peace with you. You will know that your tent is secure; you will take stock of your property and find nothing missing. You will know that your children will be many, and your descendants like the grass of the earth. You will come to the grave in full vigor, like sheaves gathered in season."

Job 8:6: "If you are pure and upright, even now He will rouse himself on your behalf and restore you to your prosperous state."

Job 11:13-15: "Yet if you devote your heart to Him and stretch out your hands to Him, if you put away the sin that is in your hand and allow no evil to dwell in your tent, then, free of fault, you will lift up your face; you will stand firm and without fear."

Job 22:23: "If you return to the Almighty, you will be restored: If you remove wickedness far from your tent . . . ."

Job 33:26: "Then that person can pray to God and find favor with Him, they will see God's face and shout for joy; He will restore them to full well-being."

275. Job 32:1.

276. Job 32:8: "But it is the Spirit in a person, the breath of the Almighty, that gives them understanding."

277. Fry, *A New Translation*, 456.

278. Ibid, 463.

*Who is this that obscures my plans with words
without knowledge? Brace yourself like a man; I will
question you, and you shall answer me. Where were
you when I laid the earth's foundation? Tell me, if
you understand. Who marked off its dimensions?
Surely you know! Who stretched a measuring line
across it? On what were its footings set, or who laid its
cornerstone—while the morning stars sang together
and all the angels shouted for joy? Who shut up the
sea behind doors when it burst forth from the womb,
when I made the clouds its garment and wrapped it
in thick darkness, when I fixed limits for it and set its
doors and bars in place, when I said, "This far you
may come and no farther; here is where your proud
waves halt?"*[279]

The Lord laid out the most magnificent and fearful aspects
of creation. He jolted Job with a panoramic view of raging
weather. In intricate detail, He described the most powerful
beasts on the planet. He pointed to the rooster, lioness, raven,
mountain goat, doe, fawn, wild ox, donkey, hawk, and eagle.
He said:

*Do you give the horse its strength or clothe its neck
with a flowing mane? Do you make it leap like a
locust, striking terror with its proud snorting? It paws
fiercely, rejoicing in its strength, and charges into the
fray. It laughs at fear, afraid of nothing; it does not
shy away from the sword. The quiver rattles against
its side, along with the flashing spear and lance. In*

---

279. Job 38:2-11.

*frenzied excitement it eats up the ground; it cannot
stand still when the trumpet sounds. At the blast of
the trumpet it snorts, "Aha!" It catches the scent of
battle from afar, the shout of commanders and the
battle cry.*[280]

Why does the author of Job dedicate so much time to describing the creatures and forces of nature? In an extraordinary analysis, the Rev. Fry answers this important question.

The expanse of creation revealed that Job's view on injustice
was based on a peephole into the universe, a minuscule
understanding of the full story. Job had acted as if he knew
it all. He was so bold that it seemed he "arrogated to himself
the knowledge and experience of such a length of days as
would have enabled him to have seen and understood all the
wonders of creation," the Rev. Fry states.[281] In fact, if we all
knew what God knew, we would see no exception to the rule
of perfect justice and goodness.[282]

Job fully believed that God would bring justice in the next
world—and thus he was able to persevere under great suffering
in expectation of a better world. It was also the reason Job was
unwilling to curse God. Such an act, he believed, would have
sent him to eternal damnation. But God's presentation of His
care for nature was intended to show Job that the very hairs
of his head were counted **on this earth.**[283]

Take, for example, the ostrich, which grows as tall as nine

---

280. Job 39:19-25.
281. Fry, *A New Translation*, 470.
282. Ibid., 463.
283. Matthew 10:30: "And even the very hairs of your head are all numbered."

feet, runs as fast as 43 miles an hour, and covers distances of 100 miles. "When she spreads her feathers to run, she laughs at horse and rider."[284] The ostrich flaps its wings joyfully,[285] allowing it to turn, stop, and provide balance. Yet, the bird does not fly. She is also careless about the welfare of her young. She lays her eggs on the ground, unmindful that a foot may crush them or that a wild animal may trample them.[286]

The Lord carefully designed the attributes of each animal, intentionally offsetting awe-inspiring strengths with weaknesses, states the Rev. Fry. "Providence, whenever it gives an extraordinary quality to an animal, gives also another to neutralize that quality, and therefore to bring it under the power of man," he writes.[287]

For mankind is the crown of creation. And the same wisdom and meticulous care that God employs in creating and maintaining millions of species applies also to the affairs of humanity.

"Will He, who in lesser things manifests so much art and design, and seems to love to put it forth so variously—will He have neglected man, or have given up His concerns to misrule; or will He act arbitrarily and without reason, in His treatment of this His noblest production? And especially in His treatment of one, to whom He has given the promise of life eternal, in

---

284. Job 39:18.
285. Job 39:13: "The wings of the ostrich flap joyfully, though they cannot compare with the wings and feathers of the stork."
286. Job 39:14-16: "She lays her eggs on the ground and lets them warm in the sand, unmindful that a foot may crush them, that some wild animal may trample them. She treats her young harshly, as if they were not hers; she cares not that her labor was in vain . . . "
287. Fry, *A New Translation*, 482.

that Redeemer whom He has revealed to Him?" the Rev. Fry asks.[288] Said differently, the evidence of God's purposeful and loving actions is nature itself, designed as a royal gift from the King of Creation to God's noblest production.

Christ said it this way: "Are not five sparrows sold for two pennies? Yet not one of them is forgotten by God. Indeed, the very hairs of your head are all numbered. Don't be afraid; you are worth more than many sparrows."[289]

The book of Job, commonly viewed as a story about the character of a righteous man, emerges instead as a story about the character of a righteous God. With hundreds of words from the Lord's own mouth, the book opens a window into God's personality. The Lord is creative, caring, humorous, logical, and wondrously forgiving.

We marvel at the manner in which the Lord conceals His holy purposes and shrewdly manages Satan. We are amused when the Lord sardonically tells Job that surely he must have been present when the earth was formed because, after all, Job knows everything. We are amazed upon learning that the Lord is offended by the same things that offend us: delusion and arrogance in religious people who mistreat others. We see Him hurt when man projects his own wrong choices onto Him, as if they were God's doing. The author of Job lays out God's magnificent creation and care of the earth. One can only imagine God's sorrow when His grand gift to mankind is abused, resulting in natural disasters that create suffering for the crown of his creation.

---

288. Ibid, 498.
289. Luke 12:6-7.

In ancient Biblical times, many people worshipped gods that were capricious, self-serving, distant, jealous, and ineffectual. In providing a window into the personality of God, the author of Job offers a stark contrast. The one true God is not far off, but extraordinarily close and mindful of each and every sorrow.

And He has a plan.

Chapter 8

TAPESTRY

*"He will yet fill your mouth with laughter
and your lips with shouts of joy."*

—BILDAD TO JOB

Job 8:21

Satan orchestrated Job's suffering—that is clear from the Scriptures —but what is also clear is that God permitted him to do so. In that sense, Job was right: God had a hand in the calamities that befell him.

The question is why? While Satan intended Job's suffering for evil, God turned the circumstances to good.

Like Job, the Patriarch Joseph was uprooted from everything he knew and loved. Based on a dream, the 17-year-old unwisely told his brothers that they would eventually bow down to him. His brothers—jealous, hate-filled, and wounded that their father loved Joseph more than them—sold the presumptuous teenager into slavery. He ended up serving the Egyptian Pharaoh, leader of the vast land. There, Joseph was falsely accused and imprisoned. Despite his sorrow and confusion, he was faithful in his day-to-day duties, and he was eventually released and restored. After earning the trust of his master, he was elevated to a position of great power— power that he used to save his brothers and many others from starving during a great famine. When their father died, his brothers feared that their powerful brother would retaliate. Joseph told them not to worry. "You intended to harm me," he said, "but God intended it for good to accomplish what is now being done, the saving of many lives."[290]

Likewise, the Lord skillfully used the cruel hate of Satan to prepare Job for his life's mission and to save many lives. While Job accused the Lord of being capricious, the Lord, in fact, had lovingly permitted a trial that was tailored to Job's potentially fatal weakness: religious pride. One might argue that God handed "this man over to Satan for the destruction of the flesh so that his spirit [would] be saved on the day of the Lord."[291] Elihu understood this when he told Job, "God sent this suffering to keep you from a life of evil."[292]

In the modernized version of the classic 17th Century book, *Let Go*, François de Salignac de La Mothe Fénelon, the Archbishop of Cambrai, France, states, "The great Physician who sees in us what we cannot see, knows exactly where to place the knife. He cuts away that which we are most reluctant to give up. And how it hurts! But we must remember that pain is only felt where there is life, and where there is life is just the place where death is needed. Our Father wastes no time by cutting into parts which are already dead. Do not misunderstand me. He wants you to live abundantly, but this can only be accomplished by allowing Him to cut into that fleshly[293] part of you which is still stubbornly clinging to life."[294]

---

290. Genesis 50:20.
291. 1 Corinthians 5:5.
292. Job 36:21 (NLT).
293. Romans 8 distinguishes between the works of the flesh, which represent the sinful state of mankind, from the works of the Spirit, which represent God, life, and peace. The latter is fueled by the power of God and, thus, is acceptable to Him; the former is not.
294. François de Salignac de La Mothe Fénelon, *Let Go*, (Springdale, PA: Whitaker House, 1973), 6-7.

The joy of Job, then, is that we do not serve an illogical or distant God. When senseless suffering barrels into our world with inexplicable force through evil hands or angry acts of nature, God restores. When catastrophe is of our own making, He forgives. When we agonize over the loss of His favor, crushed by the weight of knowing that we failed Him, God loves. During times of our rebellion, disillusionment, confusion, and straying, He waits patiently. The God who created millions of species of plants and animals understands every detail and sees every tear. Even amidst our failures and mistakes, He pursues us with relentless love. It is Satan, not the Lord, who ruthlessly accuses the repentant sinner.

God's Divine purpose in suffering may be to bring us back from the abyss through wake-up calls that—although exceedingly painful—remove the veil and show us the sobering light of reality. The trials may prevent us from being snatched from His hand. As Isaiah 38:17 says, "Surely it was for my benefit that I suffered such anguish. In Your love You kept me from the pit of destruction; You have put all my sins behind Your back."

This does not mean that every person confronted with horrific suffering requires a grand humbling or is a greater sinner than others. Christ made that clear when asked about a man born blind, whom He healed. "Rabbi, who sinned, this man or his parents, that he was born blind?" Jesus replied, "Neither this man nor his parents sinned . . . but this happened so that the works of God might be displayed in him."[295] When his followers asked Christ about the Galileans whose blood Pilate had mixed with sacrifices, Jesus answered, "Do you think that these Galileans were worse sinners than

---

295. John 9:1-3.

all the other Galileans because they suffered this way? I tell you, no! But unless you repent, you too will all perish."[296]

To the contrary, suffering can be a sign of the Lord's special affection for the one he sets his eyes on.[297] When we are willing, suffering "the trials of Job" advances us to the graduate school of knowing God, because it dismantles self-reliance, the barrier to relationship with Him, and leads to complete surrender. Only the Holy Spirit can give us the grace to see our trials this way.

Suffering can also prepare an individual for his or her life's mission to bring comfort and wisdom to others. Countless times we have seen individuals who turned their personal tragedies into hope for others facing the same trials. Often only those who have walked through the deepest darkness can break through the barriers of bitterness, fear, and confusion of those gripped by similar circumstances. Comfort offered by those unacquainted with the horrors of life's unexpected and numbing wallops can seem hollow.

Suffering may also be designed to witness to others the supernatural comfort the Lord gives to those in the throes of disaster.[298] When hurricanes hit the United States and the Caribbean in 2017, it was remarkable how many of the victims interviewed by reporters spoke of God's providence.

---

296. Luke 13:1-3.
297. Proverbs 3:12: "The Lord disciplines those He loves, as a father the son he delights in." The *Septuagint* states, "He chastens everyone He accepts as his child."
298. In 1 Peter 1:6-7, the Apostle Peter tells his readers that suffering grief in all kinds of trials is intended to prove that the genuineness of their faith—of greater worth than gold, which perishes even though refined by fire—may result in praise, glory, and honor when Jesus Christ is revealed.

After the hurricane struck Houston, Texas, the U.S. Army Corps of Engineers intentionally released waters from a dam that otherwise would have collapsed and damaged thousands of other homes. Retired Professor Daniel Cho's magnificent hand-crafted home with cathedral ceilings, finished wood walls, and a grand piano was in the path of the released waters. Later, standing in his flooded home, Professor Cho expressed deep disappointment and then said simply, "If I can sacrifice myself, and save thousands and thousands of people, maybe it's worth it. After all, God loaned it to me while I'm here, and I'm returning it."[299]

A key purpose of life's short-lived suffering is to build perseverance, character, and hope.[300] For all his human flaws, Job persevered. He did not give up or let his life slip away, as much as he was tempted to do so. Although he did not understand what was happening or why, he believed he would see God in another age. He spoke these memorable words:

> I know that my Redeemer lives, and that in the end
> He will stand on the earth. And after my skin has
> been destroyed, yet [apart from] my flesh I will see
> God; I myself will see Him with my own eyes—I,
> and not another. How my heart yearns within me![301]

In the end, Job saw God and achieved certainty in *this*

---

299. "The Houston Homes Sacrificed After Harvey," (HBO), Vice News, published on September 7, 2017.

300. Romans 5:3-5: "Not only so, but we also glory in our sufferings, because we know that suffering produces perseverance; perseverance, character; and character, hope. And hope does not put us to shame, because God's love has been poured out into our hearts through the Holy Spirit, who has been given to us."

301. Job 19:25-27.

lifetime, following much confusion and mystery. "My ears had heard of you but now my eyes have seen you," Job said, in speaking to God.[302]

By showing generations that suffering is used by God as part of His grander plan, the book of Job brings comfort that we do indeed serve a just, righteous, and, yes, eminently logical God. Romans 8:28 states, "And we know that in all things God works for the good of those who love him, who have been called according to his purpose."

It was this concept—that God uses suffering to fulfill His loving purposes and plans—that Job's friends Eliphaz, Bildad, and Zophar missed. Job had already repented for his incorrect view of God. Now it was their turn. Immediately after Job's confession, the Lord said to Eliphaz the Temanite, "I am angry with you and your two friends, because you have not spoken the truth *about Me*, as my servant Job has . . . ."[303]

What truth about the Lord was He talking about?

It could not have been what Job said before He met God, because the Lord called those statements "words without knowledge" and Job recanted them when he said, "I take back everything I said."[304]

Furthermore, Elihu spoke about Job in the same manner as the other three and God did not reprimand him.

Therefore, the Lord must have praised Job for words

302. Job 42:5.
303. Job 42:7. Emphasis added.
304. Job 42:6 (NLT).

he spoke *after he repented*—and the heart of that brief statement, a throwaway line, revolved around God's purpose and plans.[305]

> *Then Job replied to the Lord: "I know that you can do all things; no purpose of yours can be thwarted. You asked, 'Who is this that obscures my plans without knowledge?' Surely I spoke of things I did not understand, things too wonderful for me to know."*[306]

What were those wonderful things? The context of the statement suggests that Job suddenly understood the purpose for which the Lord had permitted him to suffer. Job, with all his meaningless talk, had obscured God's plans for him. Now he saw the tapestry of his life—and it was beautiful.

Have you ever wondered why a seemingly senseless event occurred, only to realize years later that it had a definite purpose and fit into a larger scheme? In the epic movie, "Prince of Egypt," the Biblical character Moses, after fleeing the palace where he was son of the most powerful ruler in the world, finds a home in a desert village, where he meets his future wife. In a simple but profoundly joyful dance, the community sings "Through Heaven's Eyes."[307] Excerpts are as follows:

> *A single thread in a tapestry, though its color brightly shines can never see its purpose, in the pattern of the grand design .... So how can you see what your life is worth or where your value lies; oh, you can never see*

305. Job 42:2.
306. Job 42:1-3.
307. Stephen Schwartz. "Through Heaven's Eyes." Copyright © Universal Music Publishing Group.

through the eyes of man, you must look at your life,
look at your life, through Heaven's eyes. Should a man
lose everything he owns, has he truly lost his worth
or is it the beginning of a new and brighter birth?

Of Job's four friends, only Elihu spoke of the concept of providence and, in doing so, escaped God's rebuke. "I will ascribe justice to my Maker . . . . [God] is mighty, and firm in His purpose," said Elihu,[308] who also spoke of God as loving.

Why is this concept of purpose so important? Because a capricious God who inflicts suffering without purpose cannot be trusted, nor can He be loving. If we believe that God acts without reason, we will go through life fearing the onslaught of senseless disaster. Who knows how an impulsive and unreliable God might whack us next?

In contrast, a logical and loving God who acts out of tremendous love for us and deep purpose can be trusted completely and unconditionally.

This does not mean we will escape suffering, as the lives of godly people attest. The Apostle Paul was beaten, stoned, whipped, and nearly drowned. He faced continual death threats. He was often hungry, cold, and exhausted.[309] The

---

308. Job 36:3-5.
309. 2 Corinthians 11:24-28: "Five times I received from the Jews the forty lashes minus one. Three times I was beaten with rods, once I was pelted with stones, three times I was shipwrecked, I spent a night and a day in the open sea, I have been constantly on the move. I have been in danger from rivers, in danger from bandits, in danger from my fellow Jews, in danger from Gentiles; in danger in the city, in danger in the country, in danger at sea; and in danger from false believers. I have labored and toiled and have often gone without sleep; I have known hunger and thirst and have often gone without food; I have been cold and naked. Besides everything else, I face daily the pressure of my concern for all the churches."

Disciples of Christ died horrible deaths. Corrie ten Boom, who spent a lifetime telling others about the wonders of God, was bed-ridden and unable to speak in her last years. In modern times, godly men and women suffer persecutions in unrelenting military conflicts that plague the earth.

If, however, we believe in a logical, loving, and purposeful God, we trust that this type of suffering will have meaning in a world in which we are only short-time visitors. We know that suffering will be used for His eternal purposes, for our good, or the good of others. Persecution of the Disciples spread the gospel and ignited a world-wide reunification of His children with God. Although its atrocities are inexplicable from a human point of view, Nazi Germany prepared countless souls to meet their Maker in eternity. The suffering of Corrie ten Boom resulted in a worldwide ministry that took her to more than 60 countries. Even in her infirmity, partially paralyzed, and unable to speak, she so exuded the presence of Christ that those near to her marveled at the obedience of the woman they called "Tante" or "Aunt" Corrie. "Tante Corrie did not fight to live, she did not fight to die. She lay in her large iron bed and took what came, not battling, but yielding. We knew this because of her attitude during the times when she opened her eyes and looked at us. Her eyes were peaceful, and they left us peaceful and with a strong sense that God was in control." So wrote her assistant, Pamela Rosewell, in the book, *The Five Silent Years of Corrie ten Boom*,[310] in one of several descriptions of why she believed the iconic woman lived in peace in her last years.

---

310. Rosewell, Pamela. *The Five Silent Years of Corrie ten Boom.* (New York, Walker and Company. Phoenix Press. Large Print Edition, 1987), 270.

Understanding that God uses the handiwork of Satan for his extraordinary pure purposes—even when they may not be immediately evident to us—brings unimaginable comfort. And that is the true lesson of Job.

That God acts compassionately with a purpose and a plan is the central theme of Job, a message intended for the ages.

But there are others.

As discussed, the story of Job establishes the dilemma of mankind and, in doing so, foreshadows the coming of Christ. God is righteous and holy. Man is proud and wicked. Righteousness requires justice, or it would no longer be righteous. Holiness cannot tolerate evil, or it would no longer be holy. To reconcile evil man and a Holy God, the book of Job prophesies the solution. Job calls for a Mediator and Redeemer. The dilemma of mankind is eventually resolved by the substitution of Christ as the sacrifice for wicked man, thus satisfying the demand of righteousness for justice. Christ atoned for the sin of man[311] to bring him back to its Creator.

The book of Job also underscores the criticality of differentiating between possessing merely an outward religion and enjoying a relationship with God. Job adhered carefully to ceremonial regulations and to selected laws such

---

311. Romans 3:23-25: "For all have sinned and fall short of the glory of God, and all are justified freely by His grace through the redemption that came by Christ Jesus. God presented Christ as a sacrifice of atonement, through the shedding of His blood—to be received by faith."

as prohibitions against worshipping idols, renouncing God, and committing adultery, but his business dealings were of concern to the Lord. The author of Job introduces us to the "new wineskins"[312] of a Spirit-filled life, one lived in a deep relationship with God, where works of the Spirit replace the powerless works of the religious flesh.

The ancient book of Job also teaches followers to shed naiveté and discern between leaders who are merely religious and those who are truly righteous, a lesson Christ forcefully reiterated when teaching his disciples to recognize the true character of the Pharisees, who loved money.[313] We should be careful about thoughtlessly projecting a label of righteous on those who claim to have good deeds under the guise of religion. Deeds and the quiet voice of the Spirit—not words, position, or attendance at Bible studies, worship services, or ceremonial events—should guide our discernment in determining what human words we accept in navigating through life's perilous journey.

Just as pride is a telltale sign of a person in Satan's grip, humility is a sign of a person in relationship with God. We are sobered through the story of Job by how easy it is to fall into delusion and how vigilant we must be in asking God to

---

312. Job 32:19: "Inside I am like bottled-up wine, like new wineskins ready to burst." Compare to Mark 2:21-22: "No one sews a patch of unshrunk cloth on an old garment. Otherwise, the new piece will pull away from the old, making the tear worse. And no one pours new wine into old wineskins. Otherwise, the wine will burst the skins, and both the wine and the wineskins will be ruined. No, they pour new wine into new wineskins."
313. Luke 16:14: "The Pharisees, who loved money, heard all this and were sneering at Jesus."

show us what we do not see. As the Psalmist says, "But who can discern their own errors? Forgive my hidden faults."[314]

The most difficult and painful voyage is the journey into one's own soul.

---

314. Psalm 19:12.

Chapter 9

THE SHREWDNESS
OF GOD

"To the faithful, You show Yourself faithful,
to the blameless, You show Yourself blameless,
to the pure, You show Yourself pure,
but to the devious, You show Yourself shrewd."

—2 SAMUEL 22:26-27

In the craft of screenwriting, dialogue is written "on the nose" or "off the nose." When dialogue is written "on the nose," the actress says exactly what she means. If she is sad, for example, she states that she is sad. In "off the nose" dialogue, however, the actress says something completely different, but the viewer infers the meaning from the context of the screenplay as a whole. If the character is sad, she may say, "I am going to the lake." And the viewer learns from watching the entire film that the lake is where she goes when she is sad. Writing dialogue "off the nose" makes a creative piece interesting and interactive by shifting responsibility onto the viewer to detect clues as to the true state of affairs.

The Book of Job uses a variation of this literary device more than four dozen times. After Job demanded the right to question God, the Lord turned the tables and forcefully issued a series of questions.

Where were you when I laid the earth's foundation? . . . . Surely you know![315]

What is the way to the abode of light? And where does darkness reside? . . . . Surely you know, for you were already born! You have lived so many years![316]

Have you ever given orders to the morning, or shown the dawn its place, that it might take the earth by the edges and shake the wicked out of it?[317]

Have you journeyed to the springs of the sea or walked in the recesses of the deep?[318]

Do you know the laws of the heavens? Can you set up God's dominion over the earth? Can you raise your voice to the clouds and cover yourself with a flood of water? Do you send the lightning bolts on their way? Do they report to you, "Here we are"?[319]

These questions and statements are rhetorical. They are not intended to be taken at face value. They are a form of writing "off the nose."

Given the overwhelming evidence that Job was not blameless, one might argue that the same literary device used at the end of the book of Job was used also in its beginning. Like bookends, the beginning and end contain dialogue that is cleverly written "off the nose."

"Have you considered my servant Job?" the Lord shrewdly asks Satan. "There is no one on the earth like him, he is

---

315. Job 38:4-5.
316. Job 38:19-21.
317. Job 38:12-13.
318. Job 38:16.
319. Job 38:33-35.

blameless and upright, a man who fears God and shuns evil."[320]

In allowing Job to suffer, the Lord was not only loving, He was shrewd. God's sleight of hand communicated to Satan only as much as He wanted Satan to know. God permitted an illusion so that He could masterfully do His work. As King David in 2 Samuel 22:26-27 says about the Lord:

> *To the faithful, You show Yourself faithful, to the blameless, You show Yourself blameless, to the pure, You show Yourself pure, but to the devious, You show Yourself shrewd.*[321]

While that theory would explain the Lord's statement to Satan in the first chapter, it would not explain the first verse in the book of Job, which describes Job as a man who was "blameless and upright; he feared God and shunned evil." This description was not part of a dialogue between God and Satan and, therefore, could not have been written "off the nose."

The description in Job 1:1 may reflect a God who lives outside time and who saw His beloved already covered in the mantle of redemption, says the Rev. Dr. Daniel Meyer, Senior Pastor of Christ Church in Oak Brook, Illinois. In that sense, the Lord saw Job for what he would become, even at the beginning. That makes the opening verse in the book "a stunning declaration of hope," the Rev. Meyer states.[322]

---

320. Job 1:8.
321. Commas were inserted to add clarity.
322. Comments were made in direct communication with the author.

A companion explanation is that the first-verse description of the man who was upright, God-fearing, and had departed from evil referred to Job *after* his trial. The Rev. Fry makes this three-part argument.

First, some theological scholars believe that the prologue to the book of Job was added by the compiler of the sacred canon after the rest of the book was written. If that is true, Job had already emerged from his trial in Verse 1.

A second indication that the description of righteousness referred to Job *after* his trial is the Arabic meaning of the name Job, which means "the man who repented and gave praise to God."[323] The Rev. Fry suggests that the name of Job before his trial was Jobab,[324] a descendant of the youngest son of Joktan, the progenitor of the ancient Arabians. Because the name Job was given *after* his repentance, the Rev. Fry reasons that the first-verse description of Job's righteousness also applied to him after his repentance.

Third, while newer translations of Job 1:1 state that Job "shunned" evil, earlier translations state that Job had *departed* from evil. The Rev. Fry cites an unnamed Bible translation that states, in the first verse of Job, "This man

---

323. Fry, *A New Translation*, 1. The Hebrew translation of Job means "persecuted," but the Rev. Fry favors the Arabic translation because Job was believed to be Arabic.

324. Ibid, 2. Genesis 10:26-30: "Joktan was the father of Almodad, Sheleph, Hazarmaveth, Jerah, Hadoram, Uzal, Diklah, Obal, Abimael, Sheba, Ophir, Havilah and Jobab. All these were sons of Joktan. The region where they lived stretched from Mesha toward Sephar, in the eastern hill country." It was not unusual for a person who underwent a transformation to gain a new name. Abraham is one example. Genesis 17:5: "No longer will you be called Abram; your name will be Abraham, for I have made you a father of many nations."

was sound and upright, and he feared Elohim, and **departed** from evil." Other translations, such as *The Revised Standard Version* and *Young's Literal Translation*, state in the first verse that Job "turned away" from evil or had been "turning aside" from evil.[325] Therefore, the very meaning of the name of Job indicates that at one point, Job had engaged in evil. Now, he was righteous and joyously praising God.

One might argue, however, that the beginning of the book of Job refers to Job's righteousness beyond the first verse and the Lord's statement to Satan. Specifically, Job 1:22 (WYC) states, "In all these things Job sinned not in his lips, neither spake any folly thing against God."

To address this argument, we are reminded that the Bible differentiates between words spoken with the lips and intentions of the heart. Romans 10:9 states, "If you declare with your mouth, 'Jesus is Lord,' and believe **in your heart**[326] that God raised Him from the dead, you will be saved." Saying the right words—verbally expressing faith—is not enough. Believing in one's heart and submitting to Him, as evidenced by the works of the Spirit, is also required. Christ reiterated this theme many times, as did James, when he said, "You believe that there is one God. Good! Even the demons believe that—and shudder. You foolish person, do you want evidence that faith without deeds is useless?"[327]

---

325. Job 1:1 (RSV): "There was a man in the land of Uz, whose name was Job; and that man was blameless and upright, one who feared God, and turned away from evil." Job 1:1 (YLT): "A man there hath been in the land of Uz— Job his name—and that man hath been perfect and upright—both fearing God, and turning aside from evil."
326. Emphases in this section were added by the author.
327. James 2:19-20.

Elihu states in Job 33:3: "My words come from *an upright heart; my lips* sincerely speak what I know." Psalm 19:14 (KJV) says, "let the words of *my mouth*, and the meditation *of my heart*, be acceptable in thy sight . . . ." Job feared that his children cursed God *in their hearts*.[328] Zophar, in seeking Job's restoration, urged Job to devote *his heart* to God.[329] The Pharisees in the New Testament were outwardly religious, but inside were unclean like "whitewashed tombs."[330]

Thus, the two remaining references to Job's righteousness refer to what Job *said*. As a religious leader, Job was well familiar with what he was expected to say, but his words may or may not have represented what he believed in his heart. The first reference, Job 1:22, states, "In all these things Job sinned not *in his lips*, neither *spake* any folly thing against God." *(WYC)*[331] The second reference, Job 2:10, states, "In all this, Job did not sin *in what he said*." What Job thought in his heart at that moment is not revealed. He may have been sincere, but the addition of the phrase "in his lips" leaves a shadow of doubt.

Job very well may have spoken from his heart in the beginning, but the feelings did not last. While Job did not charge God with wrongdoing in the first chapter, he certainly

---

328. Job 1:5: "Early in the morning he would sacrifice a burnt offering for each of them, thinking, 'Perhaps my children have sinned and cursed God in their hearts.'"

329. Job 11:13: "Yet if you devote your heart to him and stretch out your hands to him . . . ."

330. Matthew 23:27: "Woe to you, teachers of the law and Pharisees, you hypocrites! You are like whitewashed tombs, which look beautiful on the outside but on the inside are full of the bones of the dead and everything unclean."

331. Newer translations omit these three words. Emphasis added.

did later. In one of many examples, Job said, "Then know that God has wronged me and drawn his net around me."[332] The Rev. Fry believed that while Job at first bore his burden with great magnanimity, at length he gave way to despair.[333] Suffering has a way of peeling away the layers of a person until the core belief system emerges.

Satan thrives on destroying lives, while the Lord saves them. Satan is shrewd—but the Lord is shrewder. Satan would have been better off if he had permitted Job to engage in a lifetime of evil[334] and cause large numbers of people to reject the faith by permitting one more prominent religious leader who did not know God to roam the planet.

For as religious as he was, Job didn't really know God—a state to which he admitted in the end.[335] Before his epic experience, his religion was based on ceremony that he thought would win him a special place of honor and on exaggerated beliefs of his own benevolence. He spoke mightily and eloquently against the fate of wicked,[336] but turned off the soundings of his own conscience.[337] And as a hypocrite, Job might not have entered the kingdom of heaven had he not been jolted out of this delusion. "Woe to

---

332. Job 19:6.
333. Fry, *A New Translation*, 457.
334. Job 36:21 (NLT): "Be on guard! Turn back from evil, for God sent this suffering to keep you from a life of evil."
335. Job 42:5-6: "My ears had heard of you but now my eyes have seen you. Therefore, I despise myself and repent in dust and ashes."
336. Job, Chapter 27.
337. Job 27:6: "My conscience will not reproach me as long as I live."

you, teachers of the law and Pharisees, you hypocrites! You shut the door of the kingdom of heaven in people's faces," Christ said to the Pharisees. *"You yourselves do not enter, nor will you let those enter who are trying to."*[338]

Satan did not know that the Lord had a grand plan, one that intended to help—not harm—Job and those in his very large circle. In his book, *Discovering God: Fresh Vision for Longing Hearts*, the Rev. Dr. Daniel Meyer states that Satan "is desperately afraid that you will actually recognize the immense presence, the all-surpassing power of the Lord, who is closer to you right now than your own heartbeat." Using a golf analogy, the Rev. Meyer states, "Satan loathes the thought that, discovering who God is and how near He is to you, you might actually relax your white-knuckled grip on whatever club you've been using to try to prove yourself and hand it over to God. You might actually give up trying to play by your own smarts and turn to Him for coaching. You might actually become so enraptured with watching the way He handles himself that you, almost unconsciously, begin to move more and more along life's courses the way He does."[339]

Bible commentators say that the only verse of Job quoted in the New Testament[340] is I Corinthians 3:19: "As it is written: 'He catches the wise in their craftiness.'"[341] Who might the

---

338. Matthew 23:13. Emphasis added.
339. The Rev. Dr. Daniel Meyer, *Discovering God: Fresh Vision for Longing Hearts*, (Waterfall Press, a Division of Amazon, 2014), Location 549, Kindle. The Rev. Dr. Meyer is Senior Pastor at Christ Church in Oak Brook, Illinois.
340. One might argue, however, that Galatians 6:7, which states, "Do not be deceived: God cannot be mocked. A man reaps what he sows," echoes Job 4:8, which states, "As I have observed, those who plow evil and those who sow trouble reap it."
341. Job 5:13: "He catches the wise in their craftiness, and the schemes of the wily are swept away." This quote came from Eliphaz.

crafty be? Genesis 3:1 states, "Now the serpent was more crafty than any of the wild animals the Lord God had made." By reclaiming Job as his child, the Lord caught Satan— embodied by the snake[342]—in his craftiness.

Particularly poignant is what precedes the I Corinthians quote: the observation that "the wisdom of this world is foolishness in God's sight." Given how many of us have wrongly interpreted Job's character over the generations, this observation is profound and humbling.

The book of Job also offers the timeless story of forgiveness. After Job repented, Job was instructed to pray for his three friends. "The Lord said to Eliphaz, 'My servant Job will pray for you, and I will accept his prayer and not deal with you according to your folly.'"[343]

Why did the Lord give this instruction? Because while repentance is the first step toward healing, forgiveness is the second. Job and his friends needed to make amends with God, but they also needed to make amends with each other.

Job lived 140 years[344] after his devastating experience, and the Lord restored his fortunes and gave him twice as much as before.[345] In his sermon, "God will Restore All Your Wasted Years," the late Rev. David Wilkerson confessed that he "wasted" years after his book, *The Cross and the Switchblade*,

---

342. Revelation 20:2: "He seized the dragon, that ancient serpent, who is the devil, or Satan, and bound him for a thousand years."
343. Job 42:8.
344. Job 42:16: "After this, Job lived a hundred and forty years; he saw his children and their children to the fourth generation."
345. Job 42:10: "After Job had prayed for his friends, the Lord restored his fortunes and gave him twice as much as he had before."

became a worldwide hit.[346] He wined and dined with world leaders, preached to as many as 50,000 people at a time, and acquired luxury possessions. Although he did not live in flaunted sin, the fire was gone, a key evidence of which was how he treated his wife. In a sin that hinders prayers,[347] the Rev. Wilkerson was impatient with his wife when she suffered from cancer. Later filled with repentance and regret, he came to an understanding of what he called "The Law of the Harvest." Based on the Old Testament book of Joel, Chapters 1 and 2, the Law of the Harvest restores what was lost to locusts,[348] demonic powers that wither away people's joy, Wilkerson said.[349] Zechariah 9:12, too, promises to restore "twice as much" as before.[350]

One can only imagine the number of people who were blessed by the repentant Job, the greatest leader in the East, now humbled, truly wise, righteous, and living in friendship with God.

In a scene reminiscent of Charles Dickens' *The Christmas Carol* after the stingy character Ebenezer Scrooge becomes

---

346. Wilkerson, David, "God will Restore All Your Wasted Years," Published on February 23, 2016. https://www.youtube.com/watch?v=nwjdWl4m9lc
347. I Peter 3:7: "Husbands, in the same way be considerate as you live with your wives, and treat them with respect as the weaker partner and as heirs with you of the gracious gift of life, so that nothing will hinder your prayers."
348. Joel 2:25: "I will repay you for the years the locusts have eaten — the great locust and the young locust, the other locusts and the locust swarm . . . ."
349. Joel 1:12: "The vine is dried up and the fig tree is withered; the pomegranate, the palm and the apple tree—all the trees of the field—are dried up. Surely the people's joy is withered away."
350. Zechariah 9:12: "Return to your fortress, you prisoners of hope; even now I announce that I will restore twice as much to you."

transformed by supernatural confrontations into a generous man, Job and his family finally broke bread together. One can imagine the healed Job, like Ebenezer, rushing through the villages in joy to make amends to those he harmed. One can see him, moving in the flow of God's mercy and forgiveness, feeding the hungry boys living amongst the rocks. One can visualize Job restoring the widows to their homes, helping the fatherless, and losing his lifelong sense of fear. Not only was Job reconciled with his brothers and sisters, he was reconciled with "everyone who knew him before." They all ate with him in his house in what must have been a bittersweet gathering as they remembered those whose lives were lost. But the event also celebrated the healing of a great man embarking on a remarkable journey into harmony with God and his fellow human beings. It was a time for new beginnings.

INVESTIGATIVE
METHODOLOGY

As the story of Job unfolded to me, I was as stunned as anyone to see the Lord's hand draw a picture dramatically different from what I had been taught. Although painfully obvious in retrospect, the beautiful meaning of the book had been hidden from me. My new careful reading of Job was based, providentially, on a lifelong mission to gain discernment, which requires looking beyond a person's words to evaluate character, and to shed the debilitating naiveté that is so common in Christian circles. It was also based on tools and practices I employed as an investigative journalist and then as a member of the corporate investigative profession. Among them are the following.

First, I was keenly attuned to the "throwaway" lines in the book of Job. As explained in the *Introduction* to this book, I learned the value of the throwaway line from my late father, a man of few words. It is his portrait, drawn by my sister Susan Vander Wey, that graces the cover of this book and magnificently captures the joy of his old age.

One type of throwaway line is a brief, but truthful statement. Another type of throwaway line alludes to truth, but conceals the actor. This is the classic statement, "I have a friend who has a problem." An example is Job's otherwise pointless statement about the wicked, "No one criticizes them openly,"[351] which correlates to what he said about himself: "Whoever heard me spoke well of me, and those who saw me commended me."[352]

Yet another type of throwaway line refers to a place or a thing that plays a meaningful role in a scheme, but conceals what occurred. For example, a fraudster may say, "I have clients in the Cayman Islands" when, in reality, he has hidden illegal proceeds there. The islands are on his mind, so the thought comes out, but not as an admission. Job repeatedly brought up the concept of taking "security" from others, a key allegation made against him.

Investigators use these types of statements as leads on which to build a theory about what occurred. Fact-finding later confirms or dispels the theory.

A second tool of the investigative profession is examining projection. When you want to understand what a devious person is up to, look at his or her allegations against others. A classic example of this was when two prostitutes came before the Biblical King Solomon. One alleged that the other had rolled over her own baby in the night and replaced the dead baby with that of her housemate. Two people made the same allegation against the other. One was guilty. One was innocent. King Solomon used discernment to distinguish between them.[353] Job also lashed out at his friends when he

---

351. Job 21:31 (NLT).
352. Job 29:11.
353. 1 Kings 3:16-28: "Now two prostitutes came to the king and stood before him. One of them said, 'Pardon me, my lord. This woman and I live in the same house, and I had a baby while she was there with me. The third day

said, "You would even cast lots for the fatherless and barter away your friend."[354] Job offered no evidence to support this allegation, which was similar to the one that his friends made against him.

Third, investigators look for consistency in character. Job's throwaway line that the young men living among the rocks were too starved to be of economic use to him was inconsistent with his self-portrait. If Job were as benevolent to the poor as he claimed, his first reaction would be to feed those young men, not denigrate them. If he no longer had the means to help, he would have mourned over his inability to do so. Furthermore, the universal reaction of those in poverty to the rare rich man who cares for their needs would not have been one of mockery.

---

after my child was born, this woman also had a baby. We were alone; there was no one in the house but the two of us. During the night this woman's son died because she lay on him. So she got up in the middle of the night and took my son from my side while I your servant was asleep. She put him by her breast and put her dead son by my breast. The next morning, I got up to nurse my son—and he was dead! But when I looked at him closely in the morning light, I saw that it wasn't the son I had borne.' The other woman said, 'No! The living one is my son; the dead one is yours.' But the first one insisted, 'No! The dead one is yours; the living one is mine.' And so they argued before the king. The king said, 'This one says, 'My son is alive and your son is dead,' while that one says, 'No! Your son is dead and mine is alive.' Then the king said, 'Bring me a sword.' So they brought a sword for the king. He then gave an order: 'Cut the living child in two and give half to one and half to the other.' The woman whose son was alive was deeply moved out of love for her son and said to the king, 'Please, my lord, give her the living baby! Don't kill him!' But the other said, 'Neither I nor you shall have him. Cut him in two!' Then the king gave his ruling: 'Give the living baby to the first woman. Do not kill him; she is his mother.' When all Israel heard the verdict the king had given, they held the king in awe, because they saw that he had wisdom from God to administer justice."
354. Job 6:27.

Fourth, while we all labor under delusion in our lives, those in the investigative profession witness firsthand the extreme delusion of the serially destructive person. They believe they can do no wrong. They say things like, "I *am* God," or "I've done everything right," when, in reality, their lives leave a swath of destruction and pain wherever they go. It takes an incredible amount of serially destructive behavior for an entire family to abandon one of its members, particularly one who has suffered great tragedy. The abandonment of Job by his relatives was extraordinarily telling.

Fifth, we investigators know the phenomenon of the "metaview," the framework through which we see a person, one that colors our subsequent perceptions. In my profession, we see fraudsters go through great lengths to establish favorable first impressions in early interactions, often donating great sums to charity or affiliating with charitable or religious organizations to create an illusion of goodness. In Job, we accept without question the lens established for us in the beginning: that Job was righteous. It doesn't matter what Job does or says after that, what the witnesses say about him, or even that the Lord Himself accuses him: Job is righteous, because that is the lens through which we see him. Remove that metaview, and all changes.

It takes a spirit of discernment and courage to set aside the image of the respected religious pillar of the community to see darkness. It took time for Job's heart to be exposed, most of all, to himself.

Why is it so difficult to break through the metaview and see what the Rev. Fry calls "the furniture of the mind"?[355]

---

355. Fry, *A New Translation*, 96.

Because we want to believe that a religious leader, a friend, or a family member is a good person. Avoiding reality is pleasant and positive; conflict is difficult and negative, particularly in a religious setting. Furthermore, we want to follow the Biblical instructions to be kind. However, Christ did not avoid conflict. Accused of insulting the teachers of the law, He was unrelenting in his critique of them because He understood the consequences of staying silent.[356]

Furthermore, we project our situations, motives, and mindset onto others. If we suffer, we compare ourselves to Job and automatically assume we share his character traits. If we tell the truth, we think others will as well. We cannot imagine someone close to us telling outrageously grandiose lies—because we would never do that ourselves. It is much more difficult to look at actions rather than words, but "testing words"[357] is what the author of Job quietly implores us to do.

To remove the metaview of Job's righteousness, I subconsciously used a tool of the investigative profession. I began reading the book at its end—Chapter 29—a practice acquired from years of being a journalist on deadline. Reporters with no time to read a document completely before deadline begin reading at the end, because that is often where the most important information is buried. Re-reading Job without the reminder of the "metaview" of his righteousness set forth in Chapters 1 and 2 was crucial to my gaining new understanding.

---

356. Luke 11:45-46: "One of the experts in the law answered him, 'Teacher, when you say these things, you insult us also.' Jesus replied, 'And you experts in the law, woe to you, because you load people down with burdens they can hardly carry, and you yourselves will not lift one finger to help them.'"

357. Job 34:3: "For the ear tests words as the tongue tastes food."

Sixth, as an investigator, I ran a "movie in my mind" when I read the book of Job, a practice I use when conducting interviews. I visualize—step by step and in full color—what an interviewee tells me, as if I were watching a film. The gaps inform the questions I ask to fill in the missing information. So when I read that Job, as the greatest man in the East, helped every needy person, I thought of the homeless beggars in my hometown of Chicago, Illinois. I couldn't imagine a single person or organization reaching every member of this large and dispersed population, not to mention everyone with disabilities, the widows, and the orphans as well. Even large organizations miss folks. I visualized the Aurora Food Pantry, which I visited in suburban Chicago, and the massive operations it needs to fulfill its important mission. For me, comparing images of those operations to Job's self-proclaimed and universal benevolence left gaps in the movie in my mind.

Seventh, when investigators analyze allegations, we know that the level of specificity is critical. False allegations often come draped in vague conclusions without the means to obtain or verify the underlying evidence to support them. We differentiate between conclusions ("He is corrupt") and alleged facts ("He took a bribe in the corner restaurant from the operations manager of the engineering company on March 2.") Allegations that have greater credibility are those that are specific enough to be verified through evidence. Accordingly, the common belief that Job's friends harshly leveled false accusations based on *speculation* that he did something wrong does not ring true. Why? Because his friends did not say that. They did not say, "You must have done *something* terribly wrong to deserve this suffering." That allegation would have been difficult to investigate. Instead, they made very specific allegations, among them that Job, a lender or a banker, took security from his relatives without cause. This charge could be verified as either true or false through interviews with his relatives and by identification of the physical property (or people) of which Job took possession. It would also be something the entire community knew about. Although Job apparently performed his unrighteous deeds in the middle of the night,[358] word got out. In contrast to the specificity of the charges of his accusers, Job's representations about his generosity were vague. He provided no detail such as names, places, or means through which he accomplished the unbelievable feats about which he boasted.

Eighth, investigators apply mathematical-like logic in analyzing statements and events. Although generations have believed that the Lord's reprimand of Eliphaz and His commendation of Job for speaking rightly about God meant that Job was right in all that he said, that belief is not logical in light of the Lord's statement, "Who is this that obscures my plans with words without knowledge?" or in light of Job's recantation of those words. That raised for me a pressing question: what words of Job, then, did the Lord commend? To address this question, I laid out each character's statements about God on an Excel spreadsheet and looked for similarities and differences. I looked specifically for a statement made by Job and Elihu, but not by the other three friends, that

---

358. Job 36:17-20: "But now you are laden with the judgment due the wicked; judgment and justice have taken hold of you. Be careful that no one entices you by riches; do not let a large bribe turn you aside. Would your wealth or even all your mighty efforts sustain you so you would not be in distress? Do not long for the night, to drag people away from their homes."

was reinforced by the Lord himself. One statement fit the criteria: the statement that the Lord acted with a purpose and a plan. That short statement—a throwaway line—was critical because it demolished Job's argument that God acted without reason. Elihu's second singular statement, that the Lord did not despise men, complemented the first and drew a stark contrast to the capricious and unloving gods followed by many people of his day. A third statement absent in the arguments of Job's other friends was Elihu's reference to a heavenly ransom.

Ninth, investigators are keenly attuned to identifying the types of evidence that either support or discredit an allegation. Types of evidence include witness statements, suspect statements, documentary evidence, and physical evidence. In Job's case, four witnesses—and God himself—accused Job of acting unrighteously. In fact, based on their actions, not one person supported Job's view of himself. The gold standard of proof in the investigative profession is a confession given of one's free will. Job provided that when he repented in dust and ashes, took back his many words, and confessed he had only heard of God.

Finally, it is important to note that the investigative profession, while valuable in fact-finding through these and other methods, is limited to that role. It leaves prosecution to others. The ultimate Judge, our Savior, handles that matter. In the case of Job and all of mankind, the Lord created a miraculous way to wipe the slate clean. In giving us the book of Job, He provided an enduring lesson: that God loves and forgives. Job persevered amidst his confusion and delusion and, like many of us after periods of straying, finally saw the truth. Job received the chance at a do-over, he accepted it, and the man who repented and praised God undoubtedly lived in humble reverence of the Lord the rest of his life.

In the end, Job found joy.

About the Author

MARIBETH VANDER WEELE is founder of the Vander Weele Group^LLC, a Chicago-based firm that provides corporate and government investigations, intelligence, and monitoring, domestically and abroad. She served as an award-winning investigative reporter for the *Chicago Sun-Times* before joining the Chicago Public Schools as a key member of the 1995 turnaround team and subsequently as its Inspector General. In 1994, she authored, *Reclaiming Our Schools, the Struggle for Chicago School Reform*, published by Loyola University Press. She is a graduate of the political science program at Wheaton College in Wheaton, Illinois, and is a member of Christ Church of Oak Brook, Illinois.

For more information, visit:
www.joyofjob.com

Interested in Learning More?

If you would like to invite Maribeth to bring the lessons of *The Joy of Job* to your organization or learn about accompanying Bible Study materials, let us know.

WRITE
info@joyofjob.com

CALL
(773) 942-7659